COLLECTED POEMS IN ENGLISH

Books by Arun Kolatkar

ENGLISH

Jejuri (Clearing House, 1976; second edition,
   Pras Prakashan, 1978; US edition, NYRB Classics, 2005)
Kala Ghoda Poems (Pras Prakashan, 2004)
Sarpa Satra (Pras Prakashan, 2004)
The Policeman: A Wordless Play in Thirteen Scenes
   (Pras Prakashan, 2004)
The Boatride and Other Poems (Pras Prakashan, 2009)
Collected Poems in English (Bloodaxe Books, 2010)

MARATHI

Arun Kolatkarchya Kavita (Pras Prakashan, 1977)
Chirimiri (Pras Prakashan, 2003)
Bhijki Vahi (Pras Prakashan, 2004)
Droan (Pras Prakashan, 2004)
Arun Kolatkarchya Char Kavita (Pras Prakashan, 2006)

Arun Kolatkar

COLLECTED POEMS
IN ENGLISH

EDITED BY
ARVIND KRISHNA MEHROTRA

BLOODAXE BOOKS

ISBN: 978 1 85224 853 6

First published 2010 by
Bloodaxe Books Ltd,
Eastburn,
South Park,
Hexham,
Northumberland NE46 1BS.

www.bloodaxebooks.com
For further information about Bloodaxe titles
please visit our website or write to
the above address for a catalogue.

Supported using public funding by
**ARTS COUNCIL
ENGLAND**

Cover design: Neil Astley & Pamela Robertson-Pearce.

Digital reprint of the 2010 Bloodaxe Books edition.

CONTENTS

II Poems in Marathi

FROM *Arun Kolatkarchya Kavita* (1977)

FROM *Chirimiri* (2003)

EDITOR'S NOTE

Sometime in early 1967, in a Colaba Causeway bookshop in Bombay, I first set eyes on Arun Kolatkar. I had arrived in the city the previous year from Allahabad to do my MA at the university. Before coming to Bombay I had, as an undergraduate, written some poems and with two friends started a 'little magazine', a cyclostyled affair of which a couple of issues had appeared. It was called *damn you/a magazine of the arts*. I was twenty years old.

I did not know Kolatkar but had heard about him from other poets and was keen to make his acquaintance. The man in the Causeway bookshop, with his long hair, drooping moustache, large slightly hooded raptorial eyes, and distinctive clothes – five-pocket jeans, round neck t-shirt, white khadi *bundi*, fitted the mental image I had of Kolatkar, but before I could gather the courage to walk up to him and introduce myself he was gone. I must have met him soon afterwards, and either on that occasion or later I asked him for a contribution for *damn you*. He said I should come home with him, and we took a taxi from wherever we were in Flora Fountain to his flat behind the Colaba Post Office, where he lived with his first wife Darshan. It was here, without any fuss, that he gave me the manuscript of *the boatride*, each section on a separate sheet and typed in capital letters, which is how it appeared in *damn you* #6 in 1968. It was to be the last issue of the magazine. Little could I have then imagined that thirty-seven years after he gave me the poem I would be sitting by his deathbed in Pune and he would ask me to edit his posthumous book of uncollected work, *The Boatride and Other Poems*. That story is told in the Introduction; my association with him, the only 'complete man of genius' (Baudelaire's phrase for Delacroix) I've known, had come full circle. (Incidentally, the many similarities between Kolatkar's and Delacroix's 'Life and Art', as described by Baudelaire in his magnificent essay on the painter, are uncanny.)

All his life Kolatkar had an inexplicable dread of publishers' contracts, refusing to sign them. This made his work difficult to come by, even in India. *Jejuri* was first published by a small co-operative, Clearing House, of which he was a part, and thereafter it was kept in print by his old friend, Ashok Shahane, who set up Pras Prakashan with the sole purpose of publishing Kolatkar's first Marathi collection *Arun Kolatkarchya Kavita*. In the event, Shahane ended up as publisher of both Kolatkar's English and Marathi books, which together come to ten titles to date, with more forthcoming, including a newly-discovered Marathi version of *Jejuri*, a book of interviews, and a novel in English.

The small press, despite the obvious limitations, suited Kolatkar. He was, for one, in complete control of the way the book looked, from its format (he did not want his long lines to be broken), cover design, endpapers, and blurb to what went on the spine, which in the case of *Kala Ghoda Poems* and *Sarpa Satra* was precisely nothing, no title, no author's name, no publisher's logo. Moreover, with Clearing House and Pras there were no contracts to sign. From time to time, trade publishers would send Kolatkar feelers to see if he was willing to part with *Jejuri*, but making him change his mind wasn't easy. One such occasion, when he was trying to get Kolatkar to sign an earlier contract, is described by Amit Chaudhuri in his Introduction to the NYRB Classics edition of *Jejuri*, which Kolatkar gave permission for months before he died.

> At one point, I was interviewed at the inn [Wayside Inn] by a group of friends, including Shahane – a sort of grilling by the 'firm' – while Kolatkar occasionally played, in a deadpan way, my advocate. His questions and prevarications regarding the contract betrayed a fiendish ingeniousness: 'It says the book won't be published in Australia. But I said nothing about Australia.' Only my reassurance, 'I've looked at the contract and I'd sign it without any doubts in your place,' made him tranquil.

The four books that comprise the *Collected Poems in English* appear in the order in which they were published. Though *The Boatride and Other Poems* contains some of his earliest poems, it seemed proper to open a collected volume with *Jejuri*, which was Kolatkar's first book and the work he is most associated with. There comes a time in the life – or afterlife – of every cult figure when, escaping from the small group of readers that had kept the flame burning, mainly through word of mouth, he begins to belong to a larger world. With the publication of *Collected Poems in English*, Kolatkar's moment has perhaps come.

DEATH OF A POET

Arun Kolatkar, who is widely regarded as one of the great Indian poets of the last century, was born in Kolhapur, Maharashtra in 1931. His father was an educationist, and after a stint as the principal of a local school he taught at a teacher's training college in the same city. 'He liked nothing better in life than to meet a truly unteachable object,' Kolatkar once said about him. In an unpublished autobiographical essay which he read at the Festival of India in Stockholm in 1987, Kolatkar describes the house in Kolhapur where he spent his first eighteen years:

> I grew up in a house with nine rooms that were arranged, well almost, like a house of cards. Five in a row on the ground, topped by three on the first, and one on the second floor.
> The place wasn't quite as cheerful as playing cards, though. Or as colourful. All the rooms had mudfloors which had to be plastered with cowdung every week to keep them in good repair. All the walls were painted, or rather distempered, in some indeterminate colour which I can only describe as a lighter shade of sulphurous yellow.

It was in one of these rooms – his father's study on the first floor – that Kolatkar found 'a hidden treasure'. It consisted of

> three or four packets of glossy black and white picture postcards showing the monuments and architectural marvels of Greece, as well as sculptures from the various museums of Italy and France.
> As I sat in my father's chair, examining the contents of his drawers, it was inevitable that I should've been introduced to the finest achievements of Baroque and Renaissance art, the works of people like Bernini and Michaelangelo, and I spent long hours spellbound by their art.
> But at the same time I must make a confession. The European girls disappointed me. They have beautiful faces, great figures, and they showed it all. But there was nothing to see. I looked blankly at their smooth, creaseless, and apparently scratch-resistant crotches, sighed, and moved on to the next picture.
> The boys, too. They let it al hang out, but were hardly what you might call well-hung. David, for example. Was it David? Great muscles, great body, but his penis was like a tiny little mouse. Move on. Next picture.

After matriculating in 1947, Kolatkar attended art school in Kolhapur, and, in 1949, joined the Sir J.J. School of Art in Bombay. He abandoned it two years later, midway through the course, but went back in 1957, when he completed the assignments and, finally, took the diploma in painting. The same year he joined Ajanta Advertising as visualiser, and quickly established himself in the profession which, in 1989, inducted him into the hall of fame for lifetime achievement.

Kolatkar also led another life, and took great care to keep the two lives separate. His poet friends were scarcely aware of the advertising legend in their midst, for he never spoke to them about his prize-winning ad campaigns or the agencies he did them for. His first poems started appearing in English and Marathi magazines in the early 1950s and he continued to write in both languages for the next fifty years, creating two independent and equally significant bodies of work. Occasionally he made jottings, in which he wondered about the strange bilingual creature he was:

I have a pen in my possession
which writes in 2 languages
and draws in one

—

My pencil is sharpened at both ends
I use one end to write in Marathi
the other in English

—

what I write with one end
comes out as English
what I write with the other
comes out as Marathi

His first book in English, *Jejuri*, a sequence of thirty-one poems based on a visit to a temple town of the same name near Pune, appeared in 1976 to instant acclaim, winning the Commonwealth Poetry Prize and establishing his international reputation. The main attraction of Jejuri is the Khandoba temple, a folk god popular with the nomadic and pastoral communities of Maharashtra and north Karnataka. Only incidentally, though, is *Jejuri* about a temple town or matters of faith. At its heart, and at the heart of all of Kolatkar's work, lies a moral vision, whose basis is the things of this world, precisely, rapturously observed. So, a common door-step is revealed to be a pillar on its side, 'Yes. / That's what it is'; the eight-arm-goddess, once you begin to count, has eighteen arms; and the rundown Maruti temple, where nobody comes to worship but is home to a mongrel bitch and her puppies, is, for that reason, 'nothing less than the house of god.' The matter of fact tone, bemused, seemingly offhand, is easy to get wrong, and

Kolatkar's Marathi critics got it badly wrong, finding it to be cold, flippant, at best sceptical. They were forgetting, of course, that the clarity of Kolatkar's observations would not be possible without abundant sympathy for the person or animal (or even inanimate object) being observed; forgetting, too, that without abundant sympathy for what was being observed, the poems would not be the acts of attention they are.

Far from mocking what he sees, Kolatkar is divinely struck by everything before him, as much by the faith of the pilgrims who come to worship at Jejuri's shrines as by the shrines themselves, one of which happens to be not shrine at all:

> The door was open.
> Manohar thought
> It was one more temple.
>
> He looked inside.
> Wondering
> which god he was going to find.
>
> He quickly turned away
> when a wide eyed calf
> looked back at him.
>
> It isn't another temple,
> he said,
> it's just a cowshed.
>
> ('Manohar')

The award of the prize inevitably led to interviews, which, except for the interview Eunice de Souza did later, are the only ones Kolatkar ever gave. In one interview, to a Marathi little magazine that brought out a special issue on him, Kolatkar was asked about his favourite poets and writers. 'You want me to give you their names?' he replied, and then proceeded to enumerate them:

Whitman, Mardhekar, Manmohan, Eliot, Pound, Auden, Hart Crane, Dylan Thomas, Kafka, Baudelaire, Heine, Catullus, Villon, Dnyaneshwar, Namdev, Janabai, Eknath, Tukaram, Wang Wei, Tu Fu, Han Shan, Ram Joshi, Honaji, Mandelstam, Dostoevsky, Gogol, Isaac Bashevis Singer, Babel, Apollinaire, Breton, Brecht, Neruda, Ginsberg, Barth, Duras, Joseph Heller, Günter Grass, Norman Mailer, Henry Miller, Nabokov, Namdev Dhasal, Patthe Bapurav, Rabelais, Apuleius, Rex Stout, Agatha Christie, Robert Shakley, Harlan Ellison, Bhalchandra Nemade, Dürrenmatt, Arp, Cummings, Lewis Carroll, John Lennon, Bob Dylan, Sylvia Plath, Ted Hughes, Godse Bhatji, Morgenstern, Chakradhar,

Gerard Manley Hopkins, Balwantbuva, Kierkegaard, Lenny Bruce, Bahinabai Chaudhari, Kabir, Robert Johnson, Muddy Waters, Leadbelly, Howling Wolf, John Lee Hooker, Leiber and Stoller, Larry Williams, Lightning Hopkins, Andrzej Wajda, Kurosawa, Eisenstein, Truffaut, Woody Guthrie, Laurel and Hardy.

'The astonishing admixture (off the top of his head),' the American scholar of Marathi Philip Engblom has said of the list, 'not only of nationalities but of artistic genres (symboliste poetry to art film to Mississippi and Chicago Blues to Marathi *sants*) speaks volumes about the environment in which Kolatkar produced his own poetry'.

And not just Kolatkar. In the introduction to his *Anthology of Marathi Poetry: 1945-1965* (1967), in which some of Kolatkar's best-known early poems like 'Woman' and 'Irani Restaurant Bombay' first appeared, Dilip Chitre writes about 'the paperback revolution' which

> unleashed a tremendous variety of...influences [that] ranged from classical Greek and Chinese to contemporary French, German, Spanish, Russian and Italian. The intellectual proletariat that was the product of the rise in literacy was exposed to these diverse influences. A pan-literary context was created.
> [...]
> Cross-pollination bears strange fruits. [Bal Sitaram] Mardhekar wrote books on literary criticism and aesthetic theory which make references to contacts with various European works of art and literature... During his formative years as a writer, he was deeply influenced by Joyce and Eliot, and these continued to be critical influences in his critical writing throughout his career, until his untimely death in 1956.

After the success of *Jejuri*, except for the odd poem in a magazine, Kolatkar did not publish anything. To friends who visited him, he would sometimes read from whatever he was working on at the time, but there were to be no further volumes. Then in July 2004 he brought out *Kala Ghoda Poems* and *Sarpa Satra*. At a function held at the National Centre for the Performing Arts' Little Theatre in Bombay, five poets read from the two books. Kolatkar, wearing a black t-shirt and brown corduroy trousers, sat in the audience. He was by then terminally ill with stomach cancer and did not have long to live.

To his readers it must have seemed at the time, as it did to me, that the publication of these long awaited new books by Kolatkar, twenty-eight years after he published *Jejuri*, completed his English oeuvre. There were some scattered uncollected poems of course, most notably the long poem 'the boatride', but they had appeared in magazines and anthologies before and in any case were not enough to make another full-length collection. Which is why when Ashok Shahane, Kolatkar's publisher, first brought up the idea of *The Boatride and Other Poems* and asked me to draw up a list of things to include in it I was sceptical. In the event, the list, based on what was available on my shelves, did not look as meagre as I had feared. It had thirty-two poems divided into three sections: 'Poems in English', which had poems written originally in English; 'Poems in Marathi', which had poems written originally in Marathi but which he translated into English; and 'Translations', which had translations of Marathi bhakti poets, mostly of Tukaram. The first poem in the first section was 'The Renunciation of the Dog', written in 1953. A poem titled 'A Prostitute on a Pilgrimage to Pandharpur Visits the Photographer's Tent During the Annual Ashadhi Fair', from his Marathi book *Chirimiri*, was from the 1980s.

The Boatride and Other Poems, I remember thinking to myself, though small in terms of the number of pages, would be the only book to represent all the decades of Kolatkar's writing life barring the last and the only one to have, between the same covers, his English and Marathi poems. Kolatkar approved of the selection when we discussed it over the phone and made one suggestion, which was to put 'the boatride' not with the 'Poems in English', as I had done, but at the end of the book, in a section of its own. The reason for this, though he did not say it in so many words, was that in its overall structure, which is that of a trip or journey described from the moment of setting out to the moment of return, and in its observer's tone, 'the boatride', though written ten years earlier, prefigures *Jejuri*, which was his next sequence.

A week or two after this conversation when next I spoke with Kolatkar he surprised me by saying that I should edit *The Boatride*. Since the book's contents had already been decided and there were no further poems to add, or at least none that I was aware of, my role at the time, as editor, seemed limited to ensuring that we had a good copy-text. But even this, I realised, would not be easy.

There was one poem, 'The Turnaround', about which Kolatkar had in the past expressed reservation, and I wondered if I should use it as it stood. In 1989, when Daniel Weissbort and I were editing *Periplus: Poetry in Translation* (1993), I had asked Kolatkar for unpublished translations of his Marathi poems. He had shown me 'The Turnaround' on that occasion, but, unhappy about one word in it, 'daisies', had asked me not to include it in *Periplus*. The Marathi had *vishnukranta*, a common wild flower widely

16

distributed throughout India, for which he felt 'daisies' was not the right equivalent. Here is the poem:

Bombay made me a beggar.
Kalyan gave me a lump of jaggery to suck.
In a small village that had a waterfall
but no name
my blanket found a buyer
and I feasted on just plain ordinary water.

I arrived in Nasik with
peepul leaves between my teeth.
There I sold my Tukaram
to buy myself some bread and mince.
When I turned off Agra Road,
one of my sandals gave up the ghost.

I gave myself a good bath
in a little stream.
I knocked on the first door I came upon,
asked for a handout, and left the village.
I sat down under a tree,
hungry no more but thirsty like never before.

I gave my name et cetera
to a man in a bullock cart
who hated beggars and quoted Tukaram,
but who, when we got to his farm later,
was kind enough to give me
a cool drink of water.

Then came Rotegaon
where I went on trial
and had to drag the carcass away
when howling all night
a dog died in the temple
where I was trying to get some sleep.

There I got bread to eat alright
but a woman was pissing.
I didn't see her in the dark
and she just blew up.
Bread you want you motherfucker you blind cunt, she said,
I'll give you bread.

I could smell molasses boiling in a field.
I asked for some sugarcane to eat.
I shat on daisies
and wiped my arse with neem leaves.
I found a beedi lying on the road
and put it in my pocket.

17

It was walk walk walk and walk all the way.
It was a year of famine.
I saw a dead bullock.
I crossed a hill.
I picked up a small coin
from a temple on top of that hill.

Kopargaon is a big town.
That's where I read that Stalin was dead.
Kopargaon is a big town
where it seemed shameful to beg.
And I had to knock on five doors
to get half a handful of rice.

Dust in my beard, dust in my hair.
The sun like a hammer on the head.
An itching arse.
A night spent on flagstones.
My tinshod hegira
was hotting up.

The station two miles ahead of me,
the town three miles behind,
I stopped to straighten my dhoti
that had bunched up in my crotch
when sweat stung my eyes
and I could see.

A low fence by the roadside.
A clean swept yard.
A hut. An old man.
A young woman in a doorway.
I asked for some water
and cupped my hands to receive it.

Water dripping down my elbows
I looked at the old man.
The goodly beard.
The contentment that showed in his eyes.
The cut up can of kerosene
that lay prostrate before him.

Bread arrived, unbidden,
with an onion for a companion.
I ate it up.
I picked up the haversack I was sitting on.
I thought about it for a mile or two.
But I knew already

that it was time to turn around.

Apart from the problem of the copy-text, there were, in 'The Turnaround', passages I found mystifying. The poem is about a walking trip through western Maharashtra and Kolatkar gives the names of the towns he passes through: Kalyan, Nasik, Rotegaon, Kopargaon. Far from being a pleasant excursion – though it has its light moments – the trip turns out to be an ordeal. At Rotegaon, he says, he 'went on trial', but there is no mention in the poem of any crime or whether the 'dog [that] died in the temple / where [he] was trying to get some sleep' and the crime are connected. By the time he reached Kopargaon, it had become physically unendurable for him to continue walking: 'My tinshod hegira / was hotting up'. But what did 'tinshod hegira' mean? In fact, now that I was reading it with an editorial eye, I felt there was an air of mystery hanging over not just certain passages but the whole poem. '[I]n realism you are down to facts on which the world is based: that sudden reality which smashes romanticism into a pulp,' Joyce told Arthur Power. As a poet of 'that sudden reality', as someone who revelled in the particular and was passionate about nouns, especially proper nouns, Kolatkar gives us all the facts about the trip including the year ('Kopargoan is a big town. / That's where I read that Stalin was dead.'), but this only deepened the puzzle. The poem's dramatic opening line, 'Bombay made me a beggar', leaves several questions unanswered. What had made him leave the city and seek the open road? Did he have a destination in mind, or even an itinerary? Was he, as his route suggests, going to the pilgrimage town of Shirdi, which is just fourteen kilometres from Kopargaon? In 1953, the year Stalin died, Kolatkar was twenty-two years old.

My last phone conversation with Kolatkar was early in the third week of September. By then he had stopped going to Café Military, an Irani restaurant in Meadows Street, where over cups of tea he routinely met with a close circle of friends on Thursday afternoons, as he had earlier met them, for more than three decades, at Wayside Inn in Kala Ghoda before the place shut down in 2002. When his condition deteriorated, his family shifted him to Pune, to the house of his younger brother, who was a doctor. He had already been in Pune ten days when I made the phone call and found that he was too weak to speak. When I persisted, a little excitedly I'm afraid, in asking him about 'The Turnaround', he said it was 'an inner journey' and mumbled something about a 'personal crisis'. He said he'd explain everything if I came to Pune. I took the next train.

I reached Pune late in the evening of the 21st and made my way to his brother's house in Bibwewadi. The house was in a side street, a duplex in a row of identical houses, each having a modest front yard with a motor scooter or car, often both, parked in it. Kolatkar was in an upstairs room and seemed to be asleep. The brother who was a doctor was still at his clinic, but his two other brothers, Sudhir and Makarand, were there, as was his wife Soonoo. 'His mouth is constantly parched,' Sudhir said, 'and that's affected his speech. He also cannot take in any food. But he feels a little better in the mornings. Maybe you should come back tomorrow and put your questions to him.' Looking at Kolatkar, there wasn't much hope of getting answers.

When I returned in the morning, I found Kolatkar was awake and, judging by the faces of those around him, ready to receive visitors. I pulled up a chair close to his bed and we resumed the phone conversation started three days ago. Speaking haltingly and with difficulty, sometimes leaving his sentences unfinished, he said that 'The Renunciation of the Dog' and 'The Turnaround' had come out of the same experience. Though it seems from 'The Turnaround' that he went on the walking trip alone, Kolatkar said that a friend, the poet and painter Bandu Waze, had accompanied him. There is a reference to Waze, though not by name, in 'The Renunciation of the Dog':

Tell me why the night before we started
Dogs were vainly
Barking at the waves;
And tell my why in an unknown temple
Days and waves away
A black dog dumbly
From out of nowhere of ourselves yawned and leapt;
And leaving us naked
And shamefaced,
Tell me why the black dog died
Intriguingly between
God and our heads.

Kolatkar said that they spent the night before they started on the trip at the Gateway of India, which is where he heard the dogs 'vainly / Barking at the waves'. They had probably slept rough on the footpath. It would be, for them, the first of many such nights.

We know little about Waze. He and Kolatkar first met in 1952, when Kolatkar was a student at the Sir J.J. School of Art. Dilip Chitre, who was a close friend of both, describes Waze as 'a maverick, self-taught artist...with immense energy, talent, and conviction that many of his academically cultivated colleagues lacked.'

The 'academically cultivated colleagues' presumably referred to painters like Ambadas, Baburao Sadwelkar and Tyeb Mehta, who were students at the art school roughly at the same time as Kolatkar. In 1954, during the early difficult months of their marriage, when Kolatkar and his first wife Darshan Chhabda were living in Malad, Bombay, in a place that was little better than a shack, Waze moved in with them. His presence, at a time when Kolatkar had no job and practically no money of his own, couldn't have made matters easier.

Makarand, whom I asked later about the walking trip, said he was then still at school but remembered Kolatkar and Waze arriving at their father's house in Pune, unshaven and tired, looking like two sadhus. When they sat down to a meal, he said, it was as though they had not eaten in days. Indeed, accounts of eating, or more often not eating, recur throughout 'The Turnaround':

> I arrived in Nasik with
> peepul leaves between my teeth.

'The Renunciation of the Dog' does not mention the 'trial' in Rotegaon nor 'The Turnaround' the dogs at the Gateway of India, but both poems refer to the incident at the temple. In 'The Renunciation of the Dog' the incident is central to the poem ('And tell me why in an unknown temple /...A black dog dumbly,' etc), whereas in 'The Turnaround', as everything else in it, the incident, stripped down to essentials, like the language itself, is mentioned in passing.

As Kolatkar now narrated it to me, there had been a series of petty thefts in Rotegaon and the suspicion of the townsfolk fell on the two tramps. Hauled up before a group of elders (this is the 'trial' referred to in 'The Turnaround'), they had a hard time proving their innocence. When they were finally allowed to leave, it was on the condition that they first clean up the temple ('drag the carcass away') where, on the one night they had spent in it, a 'black dog' had died 'Intriguingly between / God and our heads.' Kolatkar said the dog had died at the midpoint between where they had lain down to sleep ('our heads') and the temple idol ('God').

I asked Kolatkar about 'tinshod hegira'. He said 'tinshod' referred to Nana Patil's *patri sarkar* or 'horseshoe government'. Patil was a well-known revolutionary leader during colonial times and ran a parallel government in the villages around Satara in the 1940s. Those found defying its orders and collaborating with the British had, horseshoe-fashion, tin nailed to the soles of their feet. Kolatkar, in the poem, is comparing his suffering after his hegira – or flight – from Bombay ('It was walk walk walk and walk all the way') with the suffering of those punished by Patil's *patri sarkar*. His feet felt as though 'tinshod', 'The sun like a hammer on the head'. He was by then at the end of his tether. The poem ends on a note that, in more sense than one, is visionary:

> I stopped to straighten my dhoti
> that had bunched up in my crotch
> when sweat stung my eyes
> and I could see.
>
> A clean swept yard.
> A hut. An old man.
> A young woman in a doorway.

Lying 'prostrate' before the old man was a 'cut up can of kerosene'. Kolatkar now remembered that can. It was cut in half, he said, and looked as though the old man had 'beaten the life out of it'. As he spoke, he seemed to be reliving the satoric experience of fifty years ago:

> I thought about it for a mile or two.
> But I knew already
>
> that it was time to turn around.

About the 'personal crisis', though, which had led him to re-nounce the city he was returning to, he did not say anything.

There remained the matter of 'daisies'. When I asked him about it, he said I should change it to *vishnukranta*. He had looked it up in a book on flowers, he said, but to no avail. The book didn't give the English name.

'The Renunciation of the Dog' is one of fourteen English poems, collectively called 'journey poems', written during 1953-54. Though they all came out of the same experience, the walking trip through western Maharashtra, there is nothing in the poems that identifies them with a particular landscape. It is as though, in 1953, Kolatkar had staked off his subject but not located the poetic resources to express it in. Never a man in a hurry, he was prepared to wait. The wait ended in 1967 when he wrote, in Marathi, 'Mumbaina bhikes lavla'. Its English translation, 'The Turnaround', he did in 1987, to read at the Stockholm festival.

Kolatkar showed the 'journey poems' to his friends, one of whom, Dnyaneshwar Nadkarni, who later became a well-known art critic and writer on Marathi theatre, passed them on to Nissim Ezekiel.

As editor of *Quest*, a new magazine funded by the Congress for Cultural Freedom, Ezekiel was open to submissions. He also had an eye for talent and this time, in Kolatkar, he spotted a big one. He decided to carry 'The Renunciation of the Dog' in the magazine's inaugural issue, which appeared in August 1955. It was Kolatkar's first published poem in English. Around then, he and Ezekiel also met for the first time. For someone who was to spend his next fifty years in advertising, Kolatkar's meeting with Ezekiel, fittingly enough, took place in the offices of Shilpi, where Ezekiel had a job as copywriter.

A line below 'The Hag' and 'Irani Restaurant Bombay' in Chitre's *Anthology of Marathi Poetry* says 'English version by the poet', suggesting that the two poems are translations. I knew from previous conversations with Kolatkar that he wrote them both in English and Marathi and considered them to be as much English poems as Marathi ones. Now, in Pune, as Soonoo dabbed his lips with wet cotton wool to keep them moist, he spoke about them again. The Marathi and English versions, he said, were 'very closely related'; 'they can bear close comparison'. He also said he wrote them 'side by side'. Of 'The Hag' and 'Therdi' (its Marathi title) he said he would write one line in Marathi and a corresponding line in English, or the other way round. 'They run each other pretty close.' He also commented on the rhyme scheme: 'There is no discrepancy.'

Chitre, whom I'd rung up on reaching Pune, came with his wife Viju to see Kolatkar. He had with him an office file and a spiral bound book consisting of photocopies made on card paper. He asked me to look at them. He had recently finished a short film on Kolatkar for the Sahitya Akademi, and the office file and the spiral bound book, both of which Darshan had given him, were part of the archival material he'd collected. The poems in the file consisted mostly of juvenilia, and some, with their references to 'a begging bowl' and 'the changing landscape', looked like they belonged with the 'journey poems', which, as I found out later, they indeed did:

> Destined to become a begging bowl
> We let rise our clay
> And holding it in our hand
> Wordlessly and worldlessly
> To be filled and fulfilled
> We wandered
> In the wilderness of our heart

and

> We retreated from ourselves
> To become the changing landscape
> And the mutable topography
> That accompanied us
> And whispered in our ears

I quickly went through the poems and read them out to Kolatkar. If I liked something I asked him if I could put it in *The Boatride*, and if he said yes I'd put a tick against it. The ones I ticked were 'Of an origin moot as cancer's', 'Dual', 'In a godforsaken hotel', and 'my son is dead'. The poems were typewritten and some had obvious typos. A line in 'Dual' read 'the two might declare harch thorns and live'.

'Harch'? I asked Kolatkar.

'Harsh.'

In the list I had sent him, the one he had approved of, the 'Poems in English' section had eight poems. Now it had twelve. Clearly, *The Boatride* was going to be a bigger book than I had anticipated; I also began to see why Kolatkar wanted it to have an editor.

In 1966, Kolatkar joined an advertising studio, Design Unit, in which he was one of the partners. It did several successful campaigns, including one for Liberty shirts, which won the Communication Artists Guild award for the best campaign of the year. The Liberty factory had recently been gutted in a fire and the copy said 'Burnt but not extinguished'; Kolatkar did the visuals, one of which showed a shirt, with flames leaping from it. The studio was in existence for three years and everything in the spiral bound book was from this period of Kolatkar's life. In fact, it was his Design Unit engagement diary, whose pages Darshan had rearranged and interspersed with poems, drawings and jottings. Flipping through it was like peeking into an artist's lumber-room, crammed with bric-à-brac. It revealed more about Kolatkar's public life as successful advertising professional and private life as poet than a chapter in a biography would have.

The first page had a drawing of a gladiolus, the curved handle of an umbrella sticking through the leaves. Other drawings showed an umbrella hanging from a sickle moon; from an antelope's horns; from a man's wrist; stuck in a vase; safely tucked behind a man's ear like the stub of a pencil; placed with a cup and saucer, like a spoon, to stir the tea with. The text accompanying the drawings was always the same, 'Keep it'. Between the drawings were jottings, scribbles, messages ('Darshan Kolatkar 40 Daulat Send me my green shirt'), expenditure figures ('Liquor 37.75'), memos to himself ('plan & save cost; meetings fortnightly; how to inspire/educate artists'), names and telephone numbers of clients, appointments to keep or cancel, seemingly useless scraps of paper preserved only because those who were close to him were farsighted and valued every scrap he put pen to. One page had written in it 'Ring Farooki'; 'Ring Pfizer'; 'Ring Mrs Chat. cancel 3.30 Tues. appt.'; '?Bandbox?'; '7.30 Kanti Shah'; and somewhere in the middle was also the drawing of a man with a V-shaped face and arrows for arms and legs, the right arrow-leg pointing to '12.00 Jamshed'. Against a drawing of a cut-out-like figure he had written, 'Imagine he is the client you hate most and stick a pin anywhere.' And above it, 'Just had a frustrated meeting with a frustrated client. This fellow goes on and on. I do not like long telephonic conversations. The client is a Marwari, you know.' In an invoice to one Mrs Mukati dated '9/9/67', he had jokily scribbled '10,000' under 'Quantity' and 'Good mornings' under 'Please receive the following in good order and condition'.

The scribble on the invoice, the drawings and the poems, whether early or late, are part of the same vision. Enchanted by the ordinary, Kolatkar made the ordinary enchanting. Which is why, however familiar one may be with his work, it's always as though one is encountering it for the first time. '[T]he dirtier the better' he says of the 'unwashed child' in a poem in *Kala Ghoda*, 'The Ogress', and the same might be said about the subjects he was drawn to: the humbler the better. When the ogress, as Kolatkar calls her, gives the 'tough customer on her hands', 'a furious, foaming boy', a good scrub, she has a 'wispy half-smile' on her face and 'a wicked gleam' in her eye. One imagines Kolatkar's face bore a similar expression when he mischievously transformed the humble invoice into a cheery greeting.

What can be more uninspiring, more ordinary, or, sometimes, more enchanting, than the tall stories men tell each other when they meet in a restaurant over a cup of tea? In 'Three Cups of Tea' Kolatkar reproduces verbatim, in 'street Hindi' (and translates into American English), three such stories. He wrote the poem in 1960, at the beginning of the revolutionary decade that we associate more with Andy Warhol's 1964 *Brillo Box* exhibition and the music of John Cage than with Kolatkar's poem; more with New York than Bombay. Yet the impulse behind their works is the same, to erase the boundaries between art and ordinary speech, or art and cardboard boxes, or art and fart, whose sound Cage incorporated into his music. The impulse has its origin in Marcel Duchamp's famous 'ready-mades', the snow shovels, bicycle wheels, bottle racks and urinals he picked off the peg. It was art by invoice.

By reproducing conversations heard in a restaurant in 'Three Cups of Tea', Kolatkar introduced the Bombay urban vernacular, the language of the bazaar, to Indian poetry; in 'Irani Restaurant Bombay', he introduces seedy restaurant interiors and the bazaar art on their walls.

> the cockeyed shah of iran watches the cake
> decompose carefully in a cracked showcase;
> distracted only by a fly on the make
> as it finds in a loafer's wrist an operational base.
>
> dogmatically green and elaborate trees defeat
> breeze; the crooked swan begs pardon
> if it disturb the pond; the road, neat
> as a needle, points at a lovely cottage with a garden.
>
> the thirsty loafer sees the stylised perfection
> of the landscape, in a glass of water, wobble.
> a sticky tea print for his scholarly attention
> singles out a verse from the blank testament of the table.

In 1962, when he wrote 'Irani Restaurant Bombay', Kolatkar wouldn't have read Walter Benjamin's essays, which were not then available to the Anglophone world, nor would he have heard of the arcade-haunting Parisian flâneur. But as a Bombay loafer himself, someone who daily trudged the city's footpaths, particularly the area of Kala Ghoda, he would have recognised the figure.

'Salo loafer!' says a character in Cyrus Mistry's play *Doongaji House*. Over the centuries, 'Loafer' has almost become an Indian word of abuse, suggesting a good-for-nothing who drifts through the city in self-absorbed fashion when, in fact, he is streetwise and his keen eye doesn't miss a thing. (Kolatkar himself seldom walked past a pavement bookstall without picking up a treasure.) This is true of the loafer even when he appears most relaxed, having tea, say, in an Irani restaurant, a portrait of 'the cockeyed shah of iran' displayed above the till and the whole place buzzing with flies. On these occasions, he is like a papyrologist in a library poring over a classical document, though the objects he could be studying are the tables, chairs, mirrors and bazaar prints in whose midst he sits.

The bazaar print here described – the 'stylised perfection' of the landscape – brings to mind some of Bhupen Khakhar's yet unpainted early works like *Residency Bungalow* (1969). In Khakhar's painting, the bungalow is a two-storey colonial house, complete with verandah, Doric columns and pediment; 'a lovely cottage'. Leading to it is a path, 'neat as a needle', with 'elaborate trees' on either side. In the background are more trees, painted in the same 'elaborate' fashion. In the foreground, where the 'crooked swan' might have been, is the painter's friend, Gulammohammed Sheikh, sitting very stiffly in a chair, leaning a little to his right, his arm resting on a round table. Behind him, sitting on a platform attached to the house, are smaller figures. Pop art was an influence on Khakhar, and it is not surprising that both he and Kolatkar responded to bazaar prints. They were, in their different mediums, responding to the spirit of the age.

Residency Bungalow was the house in Baroda that Khakhar and Sheikh shared, along with other painter friends of theirs. And it was from this house, which belonged to Baroda University where Sheikh taught at the art school, that Sheikh and Khakhar brought out their A4-sized little magazine *Vrischik* (1969-1973), which means scorpion in Gujarati. Among those whose work appeared in its pages was Kolatkar, who contributed translations of Namdeo, Janabai and Muktabai to a special issue of *Vrischik* (Sept-Oct 1970) on bhakti poetry. As Ezra Pound (from St Elizabeth's Hospital, Washington DC) wrote to Chak ('Dear Chak'), that is Amiya Chakravarty, '"All flows" and the pattern is intricate.'

The view from a restaurant rather than a restaurant interior is the subject of *Kala Ghoda Poems*. On most days, around breakfast time and again in the late afternoon, after the lunch crowd had left, Kolatkar could be found at Wayside Inn in Rampart Row. He would usually be alone, except on Thursday afternoons, when all those who wished to see him joined his table and there could be as many as fifteen people around it. Sometime in the early 1980s, the idea of writing a sequence of poems on the street life of Kala Ghoda, encompassing its varied population (the lavatory attendant, the municipal sweeper, the kerosene vendor, the beggar-cum-tambourine player, the drug pusher, the shoeshine, the 'ogress' who bathes the baby boy, the idli lady, the rat-poison man, the cellist, the lawyer), its animals (pi-dog, crow), its statuary (David Sassoon), its commercial establishments (Lund & Blockley) and its buildings (St Andrew's church, Max Mueller Bhavan, Prince of Wales Museum, Jehangir Art Gallery), began to take shape in his head. Asked in 1997 by Eunice de Souza, how he managed to write a poem like 'The Ogress', in which both the woman and the boy she's bathing 'emerge as complete human beings', Kolatkar replied, 'It's a secret.'* The secret, I think, lay in the gift he had of making completely impersonal the scene he was imaginatively engaging with while at the same time, eschewing all isms and ideologies, identifying closely with each part. By the time he finished the sequence in 2004, to quote Joyce's famous remark to Frank Budgen about *Ulysses*, it gave a picture of Kala Ghoda 'so complete that if it one day suddenly disappeared from the earth it could be reconstructed out of [his] book'.

The first time I heard Kolatkar read was at Jehangir Art Gallery in 1967. Two years earlier, at Gallery Chemould in the same premises, Khakhar had exhibited his first collages, their inspiration the vividly coloured oleographs that had fascinated him since boyhood. I cannot now recall what the occasion was nor, apart from the painter Jatin Das, who else read that evening, but Kolatkar read a poem that he seemed to have improvised on the spot. It began 'My name is Arun Kolatkar' and was over in less than a minute. He left immediately afterwards, making his way to one of the Colaba bars, for he was, in the late 1960s, for about two and a half years, a heavy drinker, stories of which are still told by those who knew him at the time.

To my surprise, the poem was in the Design Unit diary, written out in his neat hand. He said I could include it in *The Boatride*, then added, referring to the poem, 'It's a disappearing trick.' There were also other poems in the diary which I thought were worthy of inclusion: 'Directions', a "found" poem similar to 'Three Cups of Tea' but in a quite different linguistic register, was one and 'today i feel i do not belong', which makes the only reference to advertising in his poetry ('i'm god's gift to advertising / is the refrain of my song'), another. For the most part, though, the diary consisted of ideas for future poems ('Write a bloody poem called beer. Make it bloody.'), notes and fragments in English and Marathi, and quick verbal sketches that captured a domestic moment or something he'd seen while walking idly down a road. For Kolatkar, writing was a zero waste game; no thought that passed through his mind went unnoted.

---

* Eunice de Souza, *Talking Poems: Conversations with Poets* (Oxford University Press: Delhi, 1999), 18.

Once we got the rat behind the trunk, all we had to do was ram
it against the wall.

*

It was dark
Arun woke up
D was asleep
the sound of the ceiling fan
gets mixed up
with the sound of the elevator

*

your sulky lips are prawns
fork them with a shining smile

*

on the same tile of the footpath
where that schoolgirl is standing
a mad woman sat yesterday scratching with her nail
a rotten cunt
and a big festering wound
on her shaven head

*

Leap clear, my lion, through
the ring of fire. Mind the mane,
the hind legs and the tail.
Do it again.

I wanted to ask Kolatkar about these poems and fragments but
his voice had grown faint and he closed his eyes. It was time to
leave. As we slipped out of the room, a message came from the
kitchen downstairs that lunch was ready.

The following day, on my way to see him, I wondered if we
had not already had our last conversation. Still, in the hope that
he might be able to talk, I was carrying with me the original list
of thirty-two poems for *The Boatride*, since added to, as well as
the diary. But Kolatkar had other things on his mind.

He spoke about American popular music and its influence on
him. He said that gangster films, cartoon strips and blues had
shaped his sense of the English language and he felt closer to the
American idiom, particularly Black American speech, than to British
English. He mentioned Bessie Smith, Big Bill Broonzy and Muddy
Waters – 'Their names are like poems,' he said – and quoted the
harmonica player Blind Sonny Terry's remark, 'A harmonica player

must know how to do a good fox chase.' One reason why he liked blues, he said, was that the musicians were often untrained and improvised as they went along. He dwelt on the music's social history: how during the Depression blues performers moved from place to place, playing in honky-tonks, sometimes under the protection of mobsters. He remembered the Elton John song 'Don't shoot me I'm only the piano player'.

Blues (though it can have a spiritual side) and bhakti poetry are, in intent, markedly different from each other. One belongs to the secular world; the other addresses itself to god. There are, however, parallels between them. Each draws its images from a common pool, each limits itself to a small number of themes that it keeps returning to, and each speaks in the idiom of the street. They can sound remarkably alike.

> It's a long old road, but I'm gonna find the end.
> It's a long old road, but I'm gonna find the end.
> And when I get there I'm gonna shake hands with a friend.

could be Tukaram but is Bessie Smith, just as 'Get lost, brother, if you don't / Fancy our kind of living' could be blues but are the lines of a Tukaram song, in Kolatkar's 'blues' translation. In his use of diction, Kolatkar saw himself very much in the blues-bhakti tradition. He once said to me that he wrote a Marathi that any Marathi-speaker could follow. He also said that he was not finished with a translation until he had made it look like a poem by Arun Kolatkar.

The parallels between Kolatkar's work and blues do not end there. Here is the blues singer Tommy McClennan, standing beside a road in the Mississippi delta, waiting for a bus in the hot sun:

> Here comes that Greyhound with his tongue hanging out on the side.
> Here comes that Greyhound with his tongue hanging out on the side.
> You have to buy a ticket if you want to ride.

And here is Kolatkar in *Jejuri*:

> The bus goes round in a circle.
> Stops inside the bus station and stands
> purring softly in front of the priest.
>
> A catgrin on his face
> and a live, ready to eat pilgrim
> held between its teeth.
>
> ('The Priest')

Observe, too, the stanza unit. It was with the development of the three-line verse, which Kolatkar uses here and throughout much of *Kala Ghoda Poems*, that the blues became a distinctive poetic form.

After Elton John's 'Don't Shoot Me', Kolatkar recalled some more songs: Big Mama Thornton's 'Hound Dog' and Elvis Presley's 'Blue Suede Shoes' and 'Money Honey'. His voice, which so far had been a whisper, suddenly grew loud as he almost sang out the words:

> You ain't nothin' but a hound dog cryin' all the time.
> You ain't nothin' but a hound dog cryin' all the time.
> Well, you ain't never caught a rabbit and you ain't no friend of mine.

and

> Well, you can knock me down,
> Step in my face...
>
> Do anything that you want to do, but uh-uh,
> Honey, lay off of my shoes
> Don't you step on my blue suede shoes.

and

> You know, the landlord rang my front door bell.
> I let it ring for a long, long spell.
> I went to the window,
> I peeped through the blind,
> And asked him to tell me what's on his mind.
> He said,
>
> Money, honey.
> Money, honey.
> Money, honey, if you want to get along with me.

He said he had a record collection of about 75 LPs, which he gifted to the National Centre for the Performing Arts.

He would have gifted them, in all likelihood, in 1981, when he moved house from Bakhtavar in Colaba, where he had lived since 1970, to a much smaller one-room apartment in Prabhadevi, Dadar. Around then, he also sold off his substantial collection of music and science fiction books. The first time I visited him in Prabhadevi, I was surprised that there were hardly any books in the room. I especially missed the volumes of American and European poets, which he kept in a glass-front bookcase in Bakhtavar and which I would eye enviously each time I passed them. Those, he said, he had not sold off but because of the shortage of space had put them in storage with a friend. I remember asking if he regretted not having his books with him and he said that having them in his head was more important than their physical presence. This particular conversation with him came back to me recently while reading Susan Sontag's essay on Canetti, 'Mind as Passion'. To interpolate from it, Kolatkar's passion for books was not, as it was for Walter Benjamin, 'a passion for books as material objects (rare books, first editions).' Rather, the 'ideal' was 'to put the books inside one's head; the real library is only a mnemonic system.' To this library in the head, because of his prodigious memory, Kolatkar, at all times, had complete access. I never saw him reach out for a book, but whenever he spoke about one, whether it was a Latin American novel, *The Tale of the Genji*, or a Sanskrit *bhand*, it was as though he had it open in front of him, and if he remembered a funny passage would, while narrating it, almost roll on the floor, gently slapping his thighs.

Kolatkar may not have had space for books, but he continued to buy them as before, on a scale that would match the acquisitions of a small city library. (He purchased newspapers on the same scale too; five morning and three evening papers every day.) He bought books, read them, and passed them on to his friends. This is how I acquired my copy of Marquez's *Love in the Time of Cholera*, which he had bought in hardback soon as it became available at Strand Book Stall.

It was only a matter of time before books reappeared in his apartment, covering a wall from end to end. Scanning the titles, I found no poetry or fiction; instead, history. When, in her interview with him, Eunice de Souza remarked on the books on Bosnia on his shelves, Kolatkar dwelt at length on his reading habits:

> I want to reclaim everything I consider my tradition. I am particularly interested in history of all kinds, the beginning of man, archaeology, histories of everything from religion to objects, bread-making, paper, clothes, people, the evolution of man's knowledge of things, ideas about the world or his own body. The history of man's trying to make sense of the universe and his place in it may take me to Sumerian writing. It's a browser's approach, not a scholarly one; it's one big supermarket situation. I read across disciplines and don't necessarily read a book from beginning to end. I jump back and forth from one subject to another. I find reading documents as interesting as reading poetry. I am interested in the nature of history, which I find ambiguous. What is history? While reading it one doesn't know. It's a floating situation, a

32

nagging quest. It's difficult to arrive at any certainties. What you get are versions of history, with nothing final about them. Some parts are better lit than others, or the light may change, or one may see the object differently. I also like looking at legal, medical, and non-sacred texts – schoolboys' texts from Egypt, a list of household objects in Oxyrhincus, a list of books in the collection of a Peshwa wife, correspondence about obtaining a pair of spectacles, deeds of sale, marriage and divorce contracts. One dimension of my interest in all this is literary, for example, in the Bible as literature. The Song of Solomon goes back to Egypt and Assyria. I like following these trails.

Like all autodidacts, Kolatkar's dream was to know ('to reclaim') everything, to hold all knowledge, like a shining sphere, in the palm of the hand. Nor did he give up reading fiction altogether. One winter I was in Bombay he was reading W.G. Sebald's *Austerlitz*.

He read widely, and if a question interested him, he would track down everything there was on it. When he was contemplating a poem on Héloïse for *Bhijki Vahi* (2003), each of whose twenty-five poems is centred around a sorrowing woman – from Isis, Cassandra and the Virgin Mary to Nadezhda Mandelstam, Susan Sontag, and his own sister, Rajani, who lost her only son, a cadet pilot in the Indian Air Force, in an air crash – he collected a shelfful of books on the subject. Eventually he abandoned the idea of writing on Héloïse, saying to me that he had not been able to find a way into the story, by which he meant a new perspective on it that would make it different from a retelling. He faced a similar problem with Hypatia of Alexandria, which he solved by making St Cyril, who is thought to have had a hand in her murder, the poem's speaker.

At 393 pages, *Bhijki Vahi* (which translates as Tear-stained Notebook) is among all of Kolatkar's works the longest. It is also the most complex. Just to enumerate the books and authors he read for it is to outline a course in world literature. For 'Trimary' (Three Maries), the New Testament; for 'Laila', Fuzuli's *Leyla and Mejnun* in Sofi Huri's translation (Kolatkar said he found the introductory essay by Alessio Bombaci on the history of the poem particularly useful); for 'Apala', the *Rg Veda*, *Rg Vedic Darshan* and Chitrao Shastri's *Prachin Charitra Kosh*; for 'Isis', E.A. Wallis Budge; for 'Cassandra', Homer, Virgil, Robert Graves and Robert Payne (*The Gold of Troy*); for 'Muktayakka', the *Sunyasampadane*; for 'Rabi'a', Farid-ud-Din Attar and Margaret Smith; for 'Hypatia', Edmund Gibbon, Charles Kingsley, E.M. Forster and Maria Dzielska; for 'Po Chu-i', Arthur Waley; for 'Helenche guntaval'

(Helen's Hair), Robert Payne and Peter Green (*Alexander to Actium: The Historical Evolution of the Hellenistic Age*); for 'Kannagi', Alain Danielou's translation of *Shilappadikaram* and Gananath Obeyesekere's *The Cult of the Goddess Pattini*; for 'Nadezhda', her two volumes of autobiography and Mandelstam's prose; and for 'Susan', Susan Sontag's *On Photography*. 'Hadamma' was based on an Inuit folktale and 'Maimun', the Qureshi girl from Haryana who was the victim of an honour killing in 1997, on a clutch of newspaper reports. The story was still being reported in the Indian press when Kolatkar wrote the poem. In 'Ashru' (Tears), the first poem in the book, he uses the word 'lysozyme', an enzyme found in human tears and egg white, which he came across in a newspaper article on the work of the molecular biologist Francis Crick, and 'Kim' is a reference to Nick Ut's famous 1972 photograph showing nine-year-old Kim Phuc fleeing her village outside Saigon after a napalm attack. He does not provide the poems with notes, but had he done so, the eclecticism of his sources would be reminiscent of Marianne Moore.

Bhijki Vahi won the Sahitya Akademi Award in Marathi but otherwise the critics, daunted by its range of references, greeted it with silence. Kolatkar, unfortunately, never got round to translating its poems into English. 'Sarpa Satra', the penultimate poem in the book, appears to be an exception but it is not. I asked him about it now and he said that he started writing it in Marathi first but, compelled by the subject, also decided to write it in English. Like 'The Hag' and 'Irani Restaurant Bombay', it exists independently in both languages.

Based in the frame story of the *Mahabharata*, *Sarpa Satra* is also a contemporary tale of revenge and retribution, mass murder and genocide, and one person's attempt to break the cycle. In the story, the divine hero Arjuna decides, 'Just for kicks, maybe', to burn down the Khandava forest. In a passage of great lyrical beauty, Kolatkar describes the conflagration in which everything gets destroyed, 'elephants, gazelles, antelopes' and

> people as well.
> Simple folk,
>
> children of the forest
> who had lived there happily for generations,
> since time began.
>
> They've gone without a trace.
> With their language
> that sounded like the burbling of a brook,

34

their songs that sounded like the twitterings of birds,
and the secrets of their shamans
who could cure any sickness

by casting spells with their special flutes
made from the hollow
wingbones of red-crested cranes.

Among those who die in the 'holocaust' is a snake-woman, to
avenge whose loss her husband, Takshaka, kills Arjuna's grandson,
Parikshit. Parikshit's son, Janamejaya, then holds the snake sac-
rifice, the Sarpa Satra, to rid the world of snakes: 'My vengeance
will be swift and terrible. / I will not rest / until I've exterminated
them all.' Though the mass killing of snakes symbolically represents
the many genocides of the last century, Kolatkar, by taking a story
from an ancient epic, brings the whole of human history under
the scrutiny of his moral vision. In the *Mahabharata*, Aasitka,
whose mother is herself a snake-woman and Takshaka's sister, is
able to stop the sacrifice midway, but Kolatkar's poem offers no
such consolation:

When these things come to an end,
people find
other subjects to talk about

than just
the latest episode of the Mahabharata
and the daily statistics of death;

rediscover simpler pleasures –
fly kites,
collect wild flowers, make love.

Life seems
to return to normal.
But do not be deceived.

Though, sooner or later,
these celebrations of hatred too
come to an end

like everything else,
the fire – the fire lit for the purpose –
can never be put out.

In July 2004, as we were on our way by taxi from Prabhadevi
to Café Military, Kolatkar, looking out of the taxi window and
then at me, remarked on his English and Marathi oeuvres. With
the exception of *Sarpa Satra*, he said, his stance in 'the boatride',

Jejuri and *Kala Ghoda Poems* had been that of an observer; he was on the outside looking in. He wondered whether he'd have gone on writing the same way if he'd lived for another ten years. The Marathi books, on the other hand, were all quite different, he said, and there was no obvious thread connecting *Arun Kolatkarchya Kavita*, *Chirimiri* and *Bhijki Vahi*.

But there's something else, too, that links 'the boatride', *Jejuri* and *Kala Ghoda Poems*. Each of them is arranged in the cyclic shape of the Ouroboros, their last lines suggestingly leading to their opening ones. *Jejuri* begins with 'daybreak' and ends with the 'setting sun / large as a wheel'. Similarly, *Kala Ghoda Poems* begins with a 'traffic island' 'deserted early in the morning' and ends with the 'silence of the night', the 'traffic lights' 'like ill-starred lovers / fated never to meet'. In 'the boatride', the boat jockeys 'away / from the landing' and returns to the same spot when the ride is over. It will fill up with tourists and set off again, just as the state transport bus in *Jejuri*, at the end of the 'bumpy ride', will deliver a fresh batch of 'live, ready to eat' pilgrims to the temple priest.

His Bombay friends had meanwhile been arriving through the morning to see Kolatkar. It was a Thursday, and the crowd around his bed – Adil Jussawalla, Ashok Shahane, Raghoo Dandavate, Kiran Nagarkar, Ratnakar Sohoni – was a little like the Thursday afternoon crowd around his table at Wayside Inn. Also in the room were Dilip and Viju Chitre. Sohoni was Kolatkar's Prabhadevi neighbour and had known him since his Design Unit days. He was carrying an accordion file, bulging with papers, which he handed over to me. Separately, he also gave me a letter. It was from Edwin Frank, the editor of the *NYRB* Classics Series. Frank had been in touch with Kolatkar over *Jejuri*, which he acquired for the series in May 2004. When *Kala Ghoda Poems* and *Sarpa Satra* appeared, Kolatkar had sent him the books and Frank's letter was an acknowledgement. I read it out.

September 3, 2004
Dear Mr Kolatkar,

Many thanks for sending me *Sarpa Satra* and the long awaited *Kala Ghoda* poems. I have read both books with enormous pleasure and look forward to doing so again many times. The acuteness of description, the attentive humanity, and the humour are all extraordinary; above all, I am struck by how the poems, as true poems will, succeed in *making time* – a time in which the world becomes real and welcome and which they offer to the reader as a gift. Here's to idlis!

I also want to say how beautifully put together the two books are. And many thanks for the signed copy of Jejuri which Amit Chaudhuri has forwarded to me.

I cannot read Marathi, I am sad to say, but are there any English translations of any of the poems you have written in that language? Pras Prakashan's brief description makes me eager to find out what I can.

Where, finally, should I turn to purchase additional copies of the two new books?

With deepest appreciation and admiration,

Yours,
Edwin Frank

'Nice letter,' Kolatkar said after I finished reading it. And after a pause, 'What did you say about September?'

'September 3. It's the date on the letter,' I said.

During my visit to Bombay in July, I had told Kolatkar that I would try and visit him again in August. I couldn't go, but in anticipation of my coming he had set aside the poems which he wanted me to see, putting them in the accordion file. The first folder I pulled out from it was marked 'Drunk & other songs. Late sixties, early seventies'. This was the period when Kolatkar's interest in blues, jazz and rock 'n' roll took a new turn. He learnt musical notation and took lessons in the guitar and, from Arjun Shejwal, the pakhawaj, and started to write songs, recording, in 1973, a demo consisting of 'Poor Man', 'Nobody', 'Joe and Bongo Bongo' and 'Radio Message from a Quake Hit Town'. Three of these are "found" songs, further examples of Kolatkar's transform-ations of the commonplace. 'Joe and Bongo Bongo' and 'Radio Message from a Quake Hit Town' were based on newspaper reports and 'Poor Man' took its inspiration from the piece of paper that beggars thrust before passengers waiting in bus queues and at railway stations. It gives the beggar's life story and ends with an appeal for money. 'Poor Man' has an *ananda-lahari* in the background, an instrument that is popular with both beggars and mendicants, particularly the Baul singers of Bengal. While its plangent music is truthful to the origin of the song, the beggar's appeal, it also provides a nice contrast to the outrageous lyrics in which the 'poor man from a poor land' is an aspiring rock star, who is singing not for his next meal but because he wants 'a villa in the south of france' and 'a gold disk on [his] wall'.

In October 1973, one of Kolatkar's friends, Avinash Gupte, who was travelling to London and New York, tried to interest agents and music companies there in the demo but nothing came of the effort. Kolatkar's shot at the 'gold disk' had ended in disappointment and he abandoned all future musical plans. He filed away the 'Drunk & other songs', never to return to them again. Instead, in November-December of that year, he sat down and wrote *Jejuri*, completing it in a few weeks.

One by one, I read out the 'Drunk & other songs', many of which I was seeing for the first time. I wanted to know which ones to include in *The Boatride* and, in case there was more than one version, which version to use. I read them in the order I found them.

tape me drunk
my sister
my chipmunk

spittle spittle spittle
gather my spittle
but never in a hospital

don't tie me down
promise me pet
don't tie me down
to a hospital bed
my salvation i believe
is in a basket of broken eggs
yolk on my sleeve
and vomit on my legs

o world
what is my worth
o streets
where is my shirt

begone my psychiatrist
boo
but before you do
lend me your trousers
because in mine i've pissed

'That sounds honourable enough,' Kolatkar joked after I'd finished reading it. I read out the next one:

hi constable   tell me what's your collar size
same as mine   i bet this shirt will fit you right

the shirt is yours   feel it   don't you like the fall
all you got to do to get it is make one phone call...

'Drunk,' he said, by way of categorising the song. During his drinking days, Kolatkar had had his run-ins with the police, being picked up for disorderly behaviour on at least one occasion. Years later, he recalled the jail experience in *Kala Ghoda Poems*:

> Nearer home, in Bombay itself,
> the miserable bunch
> of drunks, delinquents, smalltime crooks
>
> and the usual suspects
> have already been served their morning kanji
> in Byculla jail.
>
> They've been herded together now
> and subjected
> to an hour of force-fed education.
>
> ('Breakfast Time at Kala Ghoda')

But the poems I was reading to him from the folder were nearer in time to the experience they described:

> nothing's wrong with me   man   i'm ok
> it's just that i haven't had a drink all day
>
> let me finish my first glass of beer
> and this shakiness will disappear
>
> you'll have to light my cigarette i can't strike a match
> but see the difference once the first drink's down the hatch

'Straight drunk,' came his response, quickly. To other songs, after hearing the first line, he said I could decide later whether to include them or not and to those towards the end he said 'Skip'. Barring two, I have included all the songs in the folder. They appear in a separate section, 'Words for Music'.

A second folder contained his translations from Marathi, six of which I had not seen before, 'Malkhamb', 'Buildings' and the four 'Hospital Poems'. In a note given on the same sheet as the poem, Kolatkar says that '*malkhamb*' 'means, literally, "a wrestler's pole". It's a smooth, wooden, vertical pole buried in the ground. A common feature found in all Indian gyms. Used by wrestlers in training and by gymnasts to display their skill.' Remembering his boyhood in Kolhapur, Kolatkar said that he used to be quite good at the *malkhamb*.

The 'Hospital Poems' were not a typescript but a photocopy from a magazine and I asked him where they'd been published. He said 'Santan'. I wondered what he meant and Adil helped me out. He said that the poems had appeared in Santan Rodriguez's magazine *Kavi*, which had brought out a special Kolatkar number in 1978.

Referring to 'The Turnaround', Kolatkar said that the book in which he'd looked for the English equivalent of *vishnukranta* was in the accordion file. 'It has a description of the flower,' he said. I hadn't had a chance to explore the file but did so now and found *Flowers of the Sahayadri* (2001) by Shrikant Ingalhalikar in one of the pockets.

'Your work is in good hands,' Adil said to Kolatkar, and repeated the sentence. He believes he saw Kolatkar smile.

Sohoni, at Kolatkar's behest, had done some photography for the cover of *The Boatride* and he showed him the pictures. They were shots of boats at the Gateway of India:

> where the sea jostles
> against the wall
> vacuous sailboats snuggle
> tall and gawky
> their masts at variance
>   islam
>   mary
>   dolphin
>
> their names appearing
>   music
>   ('the boatride')

Kolatkar looked at them without saying anything. Then Ashok Shahane asked him something to which he replied that they could discuss it once he returned to Bombay. It was the last thing he said this side of silence. He died two days later, around midnight.

Jejuri

(1976)

The Bus

The tarpaulin flaps are buttoned down
on the windows of the state transport bus
all the way up to Jejuri.

A cold wind keeps whipping
and slapping a corner of the tarpaulin
at your elbow.

You look down the roaring road.
You search for signs of daybreak in
what little light spills out of the bus.

Your own divided face in a pair of glasses
on an old man's nose
is all the countryside you get to see.

You seem to move continually forward
towards a destination
just beyond the caste mark between his eyebrows.

Outside, the sun has risen quietly.
It aims through an eyelet in the tarpaulin
and shoots at the old man's glasses.

A sawed off sunbeam comes to rest
gently against the driver's right temple.
The bus seems to change direction.

At the end of a bumpy ride
with your own face on either side
when you get off the bus

you don't step inside the old man's head.

The Priest

An offering of heel and haunch
on the cold altar of the culvert wall
the priest waits.

Is the bus a little late?
The priest wonders.
Will there be a puran poli in his plate?

With a quick intake of testicles
at the touch of the rough cut, dew drenched stone
he turns his head in the sun

to look at the long road winding out of sight
with the eventlessness
of the fortune line on a dead man's palm.

The sun takes up the priest's head
and pats his cheek
familiarly like the village barber.

The bit of betel nut
turning over and over on his tongue
is a mantra.

It works.
The bus is no more just a thought in his head.
It's now a dot in the distance

and under his lazy lizard stare
it begins to grow
slowly like a wart upon his nose.

With a thud and a bump
the bus takes a pothole as it rattles past the priest
and paints his eyeballs blue.

The bus goes round in a circle.
Stops inside the bus station and stands
purring softly in front of the priest.

A catgrin on its face
and a live, ready to eat pilgrim
held between its teeth.

Heart of Ruin

The roof comes down on Maruti's head.
Nobody seems to mind.

Least of all Maruti himself.
May be he likes a temple better this way.

A mongrel bitch has found a place
for herself and her puppies

in the heart of the ruin.
May be she likes a temple better this way.

The bitch looks at you guardedly
past a doorway cluttered with broken tiles.

The pariah puppies tumble over her.
May be they like a temple better this way.

The black eared puppy has gone a little too far.
A tile clicks under its foot.

It's enough to strike terror in the heart
of a dung beetle

and send him running for cover
to the safety of the broken collection box

that never did get a chance to get out
from under the crushing weight of the roof beam.

No more a place of worship this place
is nothing less than the house of god.

The Doorstep

That's no doorstep.
It's a pillar on its side.

Yes.
That's what it is.

Water Supply

a conduit pipe
runs with the plinth
turns a corner of the house
stops dead in its tracks
shoots straight up
keeps close to the wall
doubles back
twists around
and comes to an abrupt halt
a brass mouse with a broken neck

without ever learning
what chain of circumstances
can bring an able bodied millstone
to spend the rest of his life
under a dry water tap

The Door

A prophet half brought down
from the cross.
A dangling martyr.

Since one hinge broke
the heavy medieval door
hangs on one hinge alone.

One corner drags in dust on the road.
The other knocks
against the high threshold.

Like a memory that gets only sharper
with the passage of time,
the grain stands out on the wood

as graphic in detail
as a flayed man of muscles who can not find
his way back to an anatomy book

and is leaning against
any old doorway to sober up
like the local drunk.

Hell with the hinge and damn the jamb.
The door would have walked out
long long ago

if it weren't for
that pair of shorts
left to dry upon its shoulders.

Chaitanya

come off it
said chaitanya to a stone
in stone language

wipe the red paint off your face
i don't think the colour suits you
i mean what's wrong
with being just a plain stone
i'll still bring you flowers
you like the flowers of zendu
don't you
i like them too

A Low Temple

A low temple keeps its gods in the dark.
You lend a matchbox to the priest.
One by one the gods come to light.
Amused bronze. Smiling stone. Unsurprised.
For a moment the length of a matchstick
gesture after gesture revives and dies.
Stance after lost stance is found
and lost again.
Who was that, you ask.
The eight arm goddess, the priest replies.
A sceptic match coughs.
You can count.
But she has eighteen, you protest.
All the same she is still an eight arm goddess to the priest.
You come out in the sun and light a charminar.
Children play on the back of the twenty foot tortoise.

The Pattern

a checkerboard pattern
some old men must have drawn
yesterday

with a piece of chalk
on the back of the twenty foot
tortoise

smudges under the bare feet
and gets fainter all the time as
the children run

The Horseshoe Shrine

That nick in the rock
is really a kick in the side of the hill.
It's where a hoof
struck

like thunderbolt
when Khandoba
with the bride sidesaddle behind him on the blue
horse

jumped across the valley
and the three
went on from there like one
spark

fleeing from flint.
To a home that waited
on the other side of the hill like a hay
stack.

Manohar

The door was open.
Manohar thought
it was one more temple.

He looked inside.
Wondering
which god he was going to find.

He quickly turned away
when a wide eyed calf
looked back at him.

It isn't another temple,
he said,
it's just a cowshed.

An Old Woman

An old woman grabs
hold of your sleeve
and tags along.

She wants a fifty paise coin.
She says she will take you
to the horseshoe shrine.

You've seen it already.
She hobbles along anyway
and tightens her grip on your shirt.

She won't let you go.
You know how old women are.
They stick to you like a burr.

You turn around and face her
with an air of finality.
You want to end the farce.

When you hear her say,
'What else can an old woman do
on hills as wretched as these?'

You look right at the sky.
Clear through the bullet holes
she has for her eyes.

And as you look on
the cracks that begin around her eyes
spread beyond her skin.

And the hills crack.
And the temples crack.
And the sky falls

with a plateglass clatter
around the shatter proof crone
who stands alone.

And you are reduced
to so much small change
in her hand.

Chaitanya

sweet as grapes
are the stone of jejuri
said chaitanya

he popped a stone
in his mouth
and spat out gods

Hills

hills
demons
sand blasted shoulders
bladed with shale

demons
hills
cactus thrust
up through ribs of rock

hills
demons
kneequartz
limestone loins

demons
hills
cactus fang
in sky meat

hills
demons
vertebrated
with rock cut steps

demons
hills
sun stroked
thighs of sand stone

hills
demons
pelvic granite
fallen archways

demons

The Priest's Son

these five hills
are the five demons
that khandoba killed

says the priest's son
a young boy
who comes along as your guide
as the schools have vacations

do you really believe that story
you ask him

he doesn't reply
but merely looks uncomfortable
shrugs and looks away

and happens to notice
a quick wink of a movement
in a scanty patch of scruffy dry grass
burnt brown in the sun
and says

look
there's a butterfly
there

The Butterfly

There is no story behind it.
It is split like a second.
It hinges around itself.

It has no future.
It is pinned down to no past.
It's a pun on the present.

It's a little yellow butterfly.
It has taken these wretched hills
under its wings.

Just a pinch of yellow,
it opens before it closes
and closes before it o

where is it

A Scratch

what is god
and what is stone
the dividing line
if it exists
is very thin
at jejuri
and every other stone
is god or his cousin

there is no crop
other than god
and god is harvested here
around the year
and round the clock
out of the bad earth
and the hard rock

that giant hunk of rock
the size of a bedroom
is khandoba's wife turned to stone
the crack that runs across
is the scar from his broadsword
he struck her down with
once in a fit of rage

scratch a rock
and a legend springs

Ajamil and the Tigers

The tiger people went to their king
and said, 'We're starving.
We've had nothing to eat,
not a bite,
for 15 days and 16 nights.
Ajamil has got
a new sheep dog.
He cramps our style
and won't let us get within a mile
of meat.'

'That's shocking,'
said the tiger king.
'Why didn't you come to see me before?
Make preparations for a banquet.
I'm gonna teach that sheep dog a lesson he'll never forget.'
'Hear hear,' said the tigers.
'Careful,' said the queen.
But he was already gone.
Alone
into the darkness before the dawn.

In an hour he was back,
the good king.
A black patch on his eye.
His tail in a sling.
And said, 'I've got it all planned
now that I know the lie of the land.
All of us will have to try.
We'll outnumber the son of a bitch.
And this time there will be no hitch.
Because this time I shall be leading the attack.'

Quick as lightning
the sheep dog was.
He took them all in as prisoners of war,
the 50 tigers and the tiger king,
before they could get their paws
on a single sheep.

They never had a chance.
The dog was in 51 places all at once.
He strung them all out in a daisy chain
and flung them in front of his boss in one big heap.

'Nice dog you got there, Ajamil,'
said the tiger king.
Looking a little ill
and spitting out a tooth.
'But there's been a bit of misunderstanding.
We could've wiped out your herd in one clean sweep.
But we were not trying to creep up on your sheep.
We feel that means are more important than ends.
We were coming to see you as friends.
And that's the truth.'

The sheep dog was the type
who had never told a lie in his life.
He was built along simpler lines
and he was simply disgusted.
He kept on making frantic signs.
But Ajamil, the good shepherd
refused to meet his eyes
and pretended to believe every single word
of what the tiger king said.
And seemed to be taken in by all the lies.

Ajamil cut them loose
and asked them all to stay for dinner.
It was an offer the tigers couldn't refuse.
And after the lamb chops and the roast,
when Ajamil proposed
they sign a long term friendship treaty,
all the tigers roared,
'We couldn't agree with you more.'
And swore they would be good friends all their lives
as they put down the forks and the knives.

Ajamil signed a pact
with the tiger people and sent them back.
Laden with gifts of sheep, leather jackets and balls of wool.
Ajamil wasn't a fool.

Like all good shepherds he knew
that even tigers have got to eat some time.
A good shepherd sees to it they do.
He is free to play a flute all day
as well fed tigers and fat sheep drink from the same pond
with a full stomach for a common bond.

A Song for a Vaghya

It tore in two
when I took
this yellow scarf
from the sun.
I know it's only a half
but I'll throw it away
when I've found
a better one.

I killed my mother
for her skin.
I must say
it didn't take much
to make this pouch
I keep turmeric in.

It's my job to carry
this can of oil.
Yours to see
it's always full.
But if I can't beg
I'll have to steal.
Is that a deal?

Khandoba's temple
rises with the day.
But it must not fall
with the night.

I'll hold it up
with a flame for a prop.
Don't turn me away.
I must have my oil, mam.
Give me a drop
if you can't spare a gram.

This instrument
has one string.
And one godawful itch.
As I scratch it,
it gives me just one pitch.
But if it plays
just the one note,
who am I to complain
when all I've got
is just a one word song
inside my throat?

God is the word
and I know it backwards.
I know it as fangs
inside my flanks.
But I also know it
as a lamb
between my teeth,
as a taste of blood
upon my tongue.
And this is the only song
I've always sung.

A Song for a Murli

look
the moon has come down
to graze along the hill top

you dare not ride off with it
don't you see khandoba's brand on its flank
you horse thief

look
that's his name
tattooed just below the left collar bone

keep your hands off khandoba's woman
you old lecher
let's see the colour of your money first

The Reservoir

There isn't a drop of water
in the great reservoir the Peshwas built.

There is nothing in it.
Except a hundred years of silt.

A Little Pile of Stones

find a place
where the ground
is not too uneven
and the wind
not too strong

put a stone
on top of another
find a third
to rest on the two
and so on

choose each one
with the others in mind
each one just
the right size
the right weight

if you choose
your first stone well
the kind you can
build upon
the stones will stand

god bless you
young woman
may you be
just as lucky
as you are smart

go home now
with your husband
may you find
happiness together
and may it last

Makarand

Take my shirt off
and go in there to do pooja?
No thanks.

Not me.
But you go right ahead
if that's what you want to do.

Give me the matchbox
before you go
will you?

I will be out in the courtyard
where no one will mind
if I smoke.

The Temple Rat

The temple rat uncurls its tail
from around the longer middle prong.
Oozes halfway down the trident
like a thick gob of black blood.

Stops on the mighty shoulder
of the warrior god
for a quick look around.
A ripple in the divine muscle.

Scarce a glance
at the fierce eyes and the war paint
on the face of Malhari Martand,
and it's gone.

The temple rat blinks
as it loops down the chain hung from the stone ceiling
and its eyes shine among heavy metal links
licked by highlights.

It slips down a slope
and looks brassily over the edge
of the bigger bell
at the green sparks shaking in the glass

bangles massed in the hands
of the teen age bride on her knees,
crushing bananas on the top
of the stone linga.

And having noticed
the trace of a smile on the priest's face,
buried under a grey, week deep beard,
the temple rat

disappears in a corner of the sanctum
just behind the big temple drum.
Not a minute too soon.
Because just then the bell springs into action.

A Kind of a Cross

Tail tucked between its legs
and legs tucked under a metal plated body,
the bull calf sits on a pedestal
in the temple courtyard.

You stroke a horn. Thump him on the hump
and look up at the strange instrument of torture
that even the holy bull calf
has turned his tail upon.

It's a kind of cross that rises,
on creaky joints, above a stone platform.
It's a kind of a cross with two cross bars
you lie between and come apart,

limb from limb.
As the one with spikes and hooks
stays where it is
and the one with you on swings around.

Hills and temples dance around.
Bull calfs and tortoises swim around.
Constellations wheel overhead like vultures
in one mad carousel.

Except of course that they don't.
It's illegal.
It's the wrong time of the day
for constellations anyway.

No screaming drop of blood
firebrigades down the good wood
ten laned with time
and deepening grain.

With a fingernail, you try
to pry a rivet from the sirloin.
And hurriedly, with the ball of a thumb,
to smooth a dent from the brass rump.

The Cupboard

broken glass is held together
with bits and pieces
of an old yellowed newspaper

each rectangle
of the doorframe
is an assemblage

insecure setsquares of glass
jagged slivers thrusting down
precarious trapeziums

the cupboard is full
of shelf upon shelf
of gold gods in tidy rows

you can see the golden gods
beyond the strips
of stock exchange quotations

they look out at you
from behind slashed editorials
and promises of eternal youth

you see a hand of gold
behind opinion
stiff with starch

as one would expect
there is naturally
a lock upon the door

Yeshwant Rao

Are you looking for a god?
I know a good one.
His name is Yeshwant Rao
and he's one of the best.
Look him up
when you are in Jejuri next.

Of course he's only a second class god
and his place is just outside the main temple.
Outside even of the outer wall.
As if he belonged
among the tradesmen and the lepers.

I've known gods
prettier faced
or straighter laced.
Gods who soak you for your gold.
Gods who soak you for your soul.
Gods who make you walk
on a bed of burning coal.
Gods who put a child inside your wife.
Or a knife inside your enemy.
Gods who tell you how to live your life,
double your money
or triple your land holdings.
Gods who can barely suppress a smile
as you crawl a mile for them.
Gods who will see you drown
if you won't buy them a new crown.
And although I'm sure they're all to be praised,
they're either too symmetrical
or too theatrical for my taste.

Yeshwant Rao,
mass of basalt,
bright as any post box,
the shape of protoplasm
or a king size lava pie
thrown against the wall,

without an arm, a leg
or even a single head.

Yeshwant Rao.
He's the god you've got to meet.
If you're short of a limb,
Yeshwant Rao will lend you a hand
and get you back on your feet.

Yeshwant Rao
does nothing spectacular.
He doesn't promise you the earth
or book your seat on the next rocket to heaven.
But if any bones are broken,
you know he'll mend them.
He'll make you whole in your body
and hope your spirit will look after itself.
He is merely a kind of a bone setter.
The only thing is,
as he himself has no heads, hands and feet,
he happens to understand you a little better.

The Blue Horse

The toothless singer
opens her mouth.
Shorts the circuits
in her haywire throat.
A shower of sparks
flies off her half burnt tongue.

With a face fallen in on itself
and a black skin burnt blacker in the sun,
the drummer goes blue in the face
as he thumps and whacks the tambourine
and joins the chorus in a keyless passion.
His pockmarked half brother
twiddles, tweaks and twangs

on the one string thing.
God's own children
making music.

You turn to the priest
who has been good enough to arrange
that bit of sacred cabaret at his own house
and ask him,
                    'The singers sang of a blue horse.
How is it then, that the picture on your wall
shows a white one?'
                    'Looks blue to me,'
says the priest,
shifting a piece of betel nut
from the left to the right of his mouth.
And draws an end of a nutcracker
along the underbelly of the noble animal.
Picking on a shade of blue
that many popular painters like to use
to suggest shadow on an object otherwise white.

The tambourine continues to beat its breast.

Chaitanya

a herd of legends
on a hill slope
looked up from its grazing
when chaitanya came in sight

the hills remained still
when chaitanya
was passing by
a cowbell tinkled
when he disappeared from view
and the herd of legends
returned to its grazing

Between Jejuri and the Railway Station

You leave the little temple town
with its sixty three priests inside their sixty three houses
huddled at the foot of the hill
with its three hundred pillars, five hundred steps and eighteen arches.
You pass the sixtyfourth house of the temple dancer
who owes her prosperity to another skill.
A skill the priest's son would rather not talk about.
A house he has never stepped inside
and hopes he never will.
You pass by the ruin of the temple but the resident bitch is nowhere
around.
You pass by the Gorakshanath Hair Cutting Saloon.
You pass by the Mhalsakant Café
and the flour mill.
And that's it.
The end.
You've left the town behind
with a coconut in your hand.
a priest's visiting card in your pocket
and a few questions knocking in your head.
You stop halfway between
Jejuri on the one and the railway station on the other hand.
You stop dead
and stand still like a needle in a trance.
Like a needle that has struck a perfect balance between
equal scales
with nothing left to add or shed.

What has stopped you in your tracks
and taken your breath away
is the sight
of a dozen cocks and hens in a field of jowar
in a kind of harvest dance. The craziest you've ever seen.
Where seven jump straight up to at least four times their height
as five come down with grain in their beaks.

up   a n d   do n   a n   uP   &   d
                      w   d

      & d   u
        wo   a   p
an   n   n   a d   do   & u
d   u   an d   n   w   p
    p   d   o   &   u   n
              w   p   an d o n   a d u
            n   an n   p

d
 o   & u   n d   d w   d   p
  w   p   a   o n   n   u   an   own &
n   a   d   d   & &

an   uP   a   w
   d   d n   uP   a d   d on   a n d   a n   uP
                       n   d

Concrete poem — scattered letters spelling variations of "up", "and", "down", "&" arranged across the page:

up a n d do n a n uP & d
& d wo n a n p u a d do w & u p
d u an d p d o w n & u p an d d o n a d u p
d o w n & u p a n d d w o n n d u p an d d own & & &
an d uP a d n uP a d n d on a n d a n d uP

And there you stand forgetting how silly you must look
with a priest on your left shoulder as it were
and a station master on your right.

The Railway Station

1 *the indicator*

a wooden saint
in need of paint

the indicator
has turned inward
ten times over

swallowed the names
of all the railway
stations it knows

removed its hands
from its face
and put them away
in its pockets

if it knows when
the next train's due
it gives no clue

the clockface adds
its numerals
the total is zero

2 *the station dog*

the spirit of the place
lives inside the mangy body
of the station dog

doing penance for the last
three hundred years under
the tree of arrivals and departures

the dog opens his right eye
just long enough to look at you and see
whether you're a man a demon a demigod

or the eight armed railway timetable come
to stroke him on the head
with a healing hand

and to take him to heaven
the dog decides
that day is not yet

3 *the tea stall*

the young novice at the tea stall
has taken a vow of silence

when you ask him a question
he exorcises you

by sprinkling dishwater in your face
and continues with his ablutions in the sink

and certain ceremonies connected
with the washing of cups and saucers

the booking clerk believes in the doctrine
of the next train
when conversation turns to time
he takes his tongue
hands it to you across the counter
and directs you to a superior
intelligence

the two headed station master
belongs to a sect
that rejects every timetable
not published in the year the track was laid
as apocryphal
but interprets the first timetable
with a freedom that allows him to read
every subsequent timetable between
the lines of its text

he keeps looking anxiously at the setting sun
as if the sunset were a part of a secret ritual
and he didn't want anything to go wrong with it
at the last minute
finally he nods like a stroke
between a yes and a no
and says
all timetables ever published
along with all timetables yet to be published
are simultaneously valid
at any given time and on any given track
insofar as all the timetables were inherent
in the one printed
when the track was laid

and goes red
in both his faces
at once

5 *vows*

slaughter a goat before the clock
smash a coconut on the railway track
smear the indicator with the blood of a cock
bathe the station master in milk
and promise you will give
a solid gold toy train to the booking clerk
if only someone would tell you
when the next train is due

6 *the setting sun*

the setting sun
touches upon the horizon
at a point where the rails
like the parallels
of a prophecy
appear to meet

the setting sun
large as a wheel

Kala Ghoda Poems

(2004)

Thank you Arvind, thank you Adil,
for friendship over the years
and also for
taking a close look at the manuscript.

Pi-dog

1

This is the time of day I like best,
and this the hour
when I can call this city my own;

when I like nothing better
than to lie down here, at the exact centre
of this traffic island

(or trisland as I call it for short,
and also to suggest
a triangular island with rounded corners)

that doubles as a parking lot
on working days,
a corral for more than fifty cars,

when it's deserted early in the morning,
and I'm the only sign
of intelligent life on the planet;

the concrete surface hard, flat and cool
against my belly,
my lower jaw at rest on crossed forepaws;

just about where the equestrian statue
of what's-his-name
must've stood once, or so I imagine.

2

I look a bit like
a seventeenth-century map of Bombay
with its seven islands

not joined yet,
shown in solid black
on a body the colour of old parchment;

with Old Woman's Island
on my forehead,
Mahim on my croup,

and the others distributed
casually among
brisket, withers, saddle and loin

– with a pirate's
rather than a cartographer's regard
for accuracy.

   3
I like to trace my descent
– no proof of course,
just a strong family tradition –

matrilineally,
to the only bitch that proved
tough enough to have survived,

first, the long voyage,
and then the wretched weather here
– a combination

that killed the rest of the pack
of thirty foxhounds,
imported all the way from England

by Sir Bartle Frere
in eighteen hundred and sixty-four,
with the crazy idea

of introducing fox-hunting to Bombay.
Just the sort of thing
he felt the city badly needed.

4

On my father's side
the line goes back to the dog that followed
Yudhishthira

on his last journey,
and stayed with him till the very end;
long after all the others

– Draupadi first, then Sahadeva,
then Nakul, followed by Arjuna and,
last of all, Bhima –

had fallen by the wayside.
Dog in tow, Yudhishthira alone plodded on.
Until he too,

frostbitten and blinded with snow,
dizzy with hunger and gasping for air,
was about to collapse

in the icy wastes of the Himalayas;
when help came
in the shape of a flying chariot

to airlift him to heaven.
Yudhishthira, that noble prince, refused
to get on board unless dogs were allowed.

And my ancestor became the only dog
to have made it to heaven
in recorded history.

5

To find a more moving instance
of man's devotion to dog,
we have to leave the realm of history,

skip a few thousand years
and pick up a work of science fantasy
– Harlan Ellison's *A Boy and his Dog*,

a cultbook among pi-dogs everywhere –
in which the 'Boy' of the title
sacrifices his love,

and serves up his girlfriend
as dogfood to save the life of his
starving canine master.

6

I answer to the name of Ugh.
No,
not the exclamation of disgust;

but the U pronounced as in Upanishad,
and gh not silent,
but as in ghost, ghoul or gherkin.

It's short for Ughekalikadu,
Siddharamayya's
famous dog that I was named after,

the guru of Kallidevayya's dog
who could recite
the four Vedas backwards.

My own knowledge of the scriptures
begins
and ends, I'm afraid,

with just one mantra, or verse;
the tenth,
from the sixty-second hymn

in the third mandala of the Rig
(and to think
that the Rig alone contains ten thousand

five hundred and fifty-two verses).
It's composed in the Gayatri metre,
and it goes:

Om tat savitur varenyam
bhargo devasya dhimahi
dhiyo yonah prachodayat.

Twenty-four syllables, exactly,
if you count the initial Om.
Please don't ask me what it means, though.

All I know
is that it's addressed to the sun-god
– hence it's called Savitri –

and it seems appropriate enough
to recite it
as I sit here waiting for the sun

to rise.
May the sun-god amplify
the powers of my mind.

7

What I like about this time and place
– as I lie here hugging the ground,
my jaw at rest on crossed forepaws,

my eyes level with the welltempered
but gaptoothed keyboard
of the black-and-white concrete blocks

that form the border of this trisland
and give me my primary horizon –
is that I am left completely undisturbed

to work in peace on my magnum opus:
a triple sonata for a circumpiano
based on three distinct themes –

one suggested by a magpie robin,
another by the wail of an ambulance,
and the third by a rockdrill;

a piebald pianist, caressing and tickling
the concrete keys with his eyes,
undeterred by digital deprivation.

8

As I play,
the city slowly reconstructs itself,
stone by numbered stone.

Every stone
seeks out his brothers
and is joined by his neighbours.

Every single crack
returns to its flagstone
and all is forgiven.

Trees arrive at themselves,
each one ready
to give an account of its leaves.

The mahogany drops
a casket bursting with winged seeds
by the wayside,

like an inexperienced thief
drops stolen jewels
at the sight of a cop.

St Andrew's church tiptoes back to its place,
shoes in hand,
like a husband after late-night revels.

The university,
you'll be glad to know,
can never get lost

because, although forgetful,
it always carries
its address in its pocket.

9

My nose quivers.
A many-coloured smell
of innocence and lavender,

mildly acidic perspiration
and nail polish,
rosewood and rosin

travels like a lighted fuse
up my nose
and explodes in my brain.

It's not the leggy young girl
taking a short cut
through this island as usual,

violin case in hand,
and late again for her music class
at the Max Mueller Bhavan,

so much as a warning to me
that my idyll
will soon be over,

that the time has come for me
to surrender the city
to its so-called masters.

Parameshwari

The faint but unmistakable smell
of cheap tobacco in the air
betrays the presence of Parameshwari,

the pipe-smoking mama,
the old lavatory attendant
sitting all by herself

on the steps of a dark
and deserted Jehangir Art Gallery,
and having a quiet smoke,

a leaf pipe she herself has made
clamped between her black lips
and blacker teeth.

The Kutchi witch with the leathery face
and shrivelled dugs
may have lost her gift of prophecy;

she cannot transform herself
into a bird, for example,
kill a milchcow with a look

or turn a young onager
into a willing beast of burden,
but she is still sharp as ever

and nobody's fool.
Even with her one eye dim
and mucus-green with cataract,

she can see through the new day
and know it
for the clever forgery that it is.

Meera

1

A footloose coconut frond,
a dropout,
bored with life at the top,

with nothing to do up there
except twiddle
its three hundred fingers

all day long and through the night,
or tickle the moon
now and then,

and looking for something
a little more interesting and/or
useful to do,

has befriended
and attached itself
to Our Lady of Dead Flowers,

the sad-eyed feminine half
of the municipal street-cleaning team
in this part of town.

It's learning new tricks
in her hand,
at her bidding,

and is having
altogether a great time
in the bargain.

2

She, in turn,
finds it more lively, more fun,
and just as – if not more – effective,

with its longer reach and wider sweep,
than the regular broomstick,
the fan-tail type, that comes with the job,

which she finds much too stiff and unbending,
though it's preferred by her partner,
the man she works in tandem with.

It's a joy to see the coconut frond
clown around, jump and dance
like a performing bear, a green one.

It runs ahead of her,
crossing and recrossing her path,
clearing the road before her;

it circles around her,
vaults over her from side to side,
stops when she stops;

it lunges and takes sideswipes
at errant scraps of paper,
chases the riffraff of dry leaves off the road.

3

When most art critics are still in bed,
sleeping off
the effects of last night's free drinks,

with the cache of cashew nuts
they squirrelled away
still in their pockets,

a fresh new series of installations
goes on display
in front of the Jehangir Art Gallery

– still sleeping with its mouth
open, as usual –
with no fanfare, and unseen by any

save a few discerning crows and a kitten,
in the form of modest piles of rubbish
all along the kerb

at regular intervals of about
fifteen paces perhaps,
and consisting of dry leaves, scraps of paper,

prawn shells, onion skins, potato peels,
castoff condoms, dead flowers
– mostly gulmohur and copper-pod.

The installations might as well have been
titled 'Homage to Bombay, one',
'Homage to Bombay, two' and so on,

since a good bit of the city stands
on sweepings such as these.
All of Colaba, for example, or Khetwadi.

4

The exhibition is open
for no more than about half an hour
every morning.

By the time the last pile of rubbish
has been lovingly put together,
the first one is ready for the trolley.

Which is the whole point, really.
To celebrate
the essential impermanence of all art.

5

Euclid would've loved it
– that rickety looking rattletrap,
that garbage trolley.

The honey cart,
that looks like a theorem picked
clean of proof,

has all the starkness
and simplicity of a child's drawing
done in black crayon.

It's a wrought-iron tray
that cradles two wicker bins the size
of laundry baskets

held in place by two
equilateral triangles on either side.
It stays close to the ground

and trundles along
as it moves like rolling thunder
on two iron wheels with naked rims

when pushed like a pram,
and has the decency to shudder
at the noise it makes;

dreaming the while of the softer,
more hoof-friendly roads of Mayhew's London,
for which it must've been designed.

I won't be surprised
if that tireless fossil belongs
to the very first

generation of trolleys
that came to these shores way back
in 1872 or some such date,

with the noble mission
of cleaning this city.
A difficult enough job

at the best of times,
made well-nigh impossible
by the fact

that more and more of Bombay
keeps mushrooming
on land wrested from the sea,

the malarial swamps,
salt marshes
and creeks that surround it,

and reclaimed by sweepings,
such as this trolley collects
day after day;

with the result, that
the more you clean Bombay
the more Bombay there is to clean.

6

When it is full
nearly to the brim,
she climbs to the top

and begins to dance
within the narrow compass
of the wicker bin

like a Meera before her Lord,
a Meera
with a broomstick for a lute;

shifting her weight
from one foot to the other,
she turns around herself

by slow degrees,
giving her toes
enough time

to genuflect and offer
obeisance
to all the cardinal points,

to each of
the thirty-two compass points,
in turn.

Her free arm, raised
in the air,
is a flamingo in flight.

7

Bearing down
on the load of rubbish,
treading it down

to compact it
and make room for more,
with skilled feet

she tramples it
like a vineyard wench
in a tub of grapes.

As they sink deeper
into themselves,
eggshells and dead flowers,

dry leaves and melon rinds,
breadcrumbs and condoms,
chicken bones and potato peels

start giving of their essence,
exude the wine
of worthlessness, express

an attar of thankfulness
that floods
the cracks on her heels,

licks the soles
and arches of her feet,
anoints

calluses,
and rises
between her toes.

Song of Rubbish

Grapes,
as vineyard wenches crush them underfoot,
aspire to greater glory,

after more penance,
and a period of silence and seclusion
in a dark cellar.

Clay,
as a potter treads it, hopes to rise again,
find a new purpose

and sit,
cheek to cheek, on a pretty maiden's shoulder,
after being tested in fire.

We too
have our own tryst with destiny, and feel
the birth-pangs of a new

city,
but prepare for a long period of exile
in the wilderness of a landfill

site.

A Note on the Reproductive Cycle of Rubbish

It may not look like much.
But watch out
when rubbish meets rubbish

in the back of a truck,
and more rubbish
in a whole caravan of trucks,

and then some more
in a vast landfill site
where it matures.

Rubbish ovulates
only once
in its lifetime,

releasing pheromones
during the period
of its fertility.

Driven wild by the scent,
speculators in rut
arrive on the scene in droves,

their chequebooks hanging out,
and slug it out
among themselves.

Rubbish waits.
Patiently.
And copulates with the winner.

To a Crow

That was smooth,
Mr Crow
– a perfect landing.

You swoop down
from the Y axis of the tree
(a black blur in free fall),

stretch your wings
and level off
along the baseline of the pavement,

executing
a perfect hyperbolic curve
with throwaway ease,

until you just skim along,
give yourself a slight lift,
and touch down.

Oh, that was just beautifully done
– you, you, you
airdevil!

And you did it just right;
you landed
a twiglength away from it.

Because you can't
just jump on it with both your feet, you know,
as you would on a dead rat.

And you can't just walk right up to it
and pick it up either.
No no no no no.

The frontal approach will never do;
this is a delicate matter.
You can't afford to let your interest show.

You saw it first. Sure,
but does it belong to anyone?
Look around carefully.

Is there anyone in sight
who looks like he may have
a legal claim to it?

What about that bearded man
with a briefcase in his hand?
Does he have an eye on it, you think?

What about the lady lawyer
accompanying him?
No, they're just waiting for a taxi.

Sneak a look at it.
It's not just a crack in the pavement, is it?
Are you sure?

And it's not about to crawl away either, is it?
Well then – now.
Tactfully, tactfully.

Move sideways, without looking at it.
Not all at once, but in two steps;
a side-shuffle, more like.

And there you are.
NOW!
Stand on it.

A twig! A twig! A twig! A twig! A twig!
You got it! You got it! You got it!
It's all yours, now.

You can take it away
any time you want.
But first, examine it.

Bite it.
Is it going to bite you back?
Pick it up and drop it down.

Caw!
Is it too long, too short, too thick, too thin?
Too crooked, too straight?

Is it forked?
And if so,
is it too acute or too obtuse?

What about the balance, is the balance just right?
Is it too rotten, too brittle, too limp, too stiff, too heavy, too light?
Is it naked or insulated?

Does it shine? Does it sing?
Does it spark and crackle? Does it sting?
Does it scan? Does it rhyme?

Does it make sense;
and, if it does, what does it mean?
Ask yourself,

Will it fit in with the rest?
Is this precisely the twig you need for your nest
at precisely this moment?

And, above all, do you like it?
And what about your wife?
Will she like it?

Or won't she?
Or will she laugh outright in your face
and ask you to start building your nest again – from scratch?

The Ogress

One side of her face
(the right one)
is human enough;

but the other,
where the muscles are all
fused together,

burnt perhaps,
or melted down with acid
– I don't know which –

is all scar tissue
and looks
more like a side of bacon.

*

The one-eyed ogress
of Rope Walk Lane
(one breast removed,

hysterectomised,
a crown of close-cropped
moth-eaten hair,

gray,
on a head half-covered
in a scarecrow sari)

has always been a kind
of an auxiliary mother,
semi-official nanny

and baby-bather-in-chief
to a whole chain of children
born to this street.

*

Give her a bucket filled with water,
a bit of soap
and an unwashed child

– the dirtier the better –
and the wispy half-smile
that always plays

on the good side of her face
loses
its unfinished look

without completing itself;
and she gets a wicked gleam
in her right eye

as she starts unwrapping her gift
– the naughtier the better –
and she is never so happy

as when she has
a tough customer on her hands,
and she has whisked

his nappy off
– like now,
for example.

*

Soap in eye,
a furious, foaming boy
– very angry,

very wet –
cradled lengthwise
and face down

on her spindly legs,
extended jointly
and straight out before her,

she sits on the edge
of the pavement; facing the road,
sari pulled up to her crotch,

and her instruments of torture
within easy reach:
an empty, sky-blue plastic mug

bobbing up and down
gleefully
in a bucket full of water.

*

As grown-up fingers soap him,
grab ass,
scrub and knead his flesh,

the headlong boy,
end-stopped by the woman's feet
pointing skyward,

nose down between her ankles,
and restricted
by her no-win shins,

is overrun by swirling
galaxies of backsliding
foam that collide

form and re-form,
slither up and down
and wrap around

the curved space
of his slippery body,
black as wet slate.

*

She turns him on his flip side
and, face clenched,
he kicks her in the crotch;

starts bawling
and shaking his fists
at the world;

but she grabs both his feet
with one hand,
crumples his face,

pulls his ears,
tweaks his nose,
probes his nostrils,

twists his arms,
polishes his balls,
plays with his pintle

and hits him
with three mugs full
of cold water

in quick succession.

*

The water cascades down his sides;
it sluices down her legs
that form a bridge

over a lengthening river
of bath water
flowing down the kerbside

like frothing star-broth
that will be swallowed up
by a rat-hole

waiting for it
further downstream.

*

And, after the flood,
when the ogress lifts him up in the air
and sets him down

on solid ground
– dripping wet
but all in one piece –

feeling a bit like a little Noah,
bow-legged and tottering,
he stands,

supported by an adult hand
under an armpit,
but still

on his own two feet,
and a street-fighting man
already.

*

When the ogress throws
a towel over him
and starts drying him,

he nods unsteadily
– for he is still not quite able
to balance his head –

looks around
at the whole honking world
that has massed its buildings

menacingly around him
and he already knows –
what his response is going to be.

He points his little
water cannon
at the world in general

and (Right!
Piss on it, boy)
shoots a perfect arc of piss,

lusty
and luminous
in the morning sun.

Silver Triangle

1

Three kerbstones,
each about a span in length,
completely smothered
under her enormous fanny

that resembles
a slightly depressed looking
iron wrecking-ball
more than anything else

(a little mellowed with age, perhaps,
though it doesn't seem to have lost
any of its clout
or patability);

and a pensive finger,
blackened with
Monkey Brand Tooth Powder,
stuck inside her mouth,

neatly plugged into a socket
cleverly concealed
between a golden molar
and a cheek,

that gives her direct access
to a secret chamber of her brain;
your granny is sitting
on the pavement's edge

trying to remember
a funny dream she had last night,
with a faraway look
in her eyes,

and a black pearl of drool
poised precariously
on the knuckle
of her index finger.

2

Your various aunts
are playing a game of cards,
rummy,
under the mahogany.

Across the road,
a conference of sorts
seems to be in progress
– between your mum,

a crooked cop
and an equally crooked lamp-post;
and, what with one thing
and another,

no one's had the time yet,
obviously,
to do your hair this morning,
or bother with you in any way.

That droopy ribbon, for instance,
has been steadily losing its hold
on what used to be
a pigtail.

The way it's still hanging in there
is nothing short of a miracle
(it wasn't going to last
– you dropped it).

But, in spite of everything,
brat fatale,
I must say you're looking fine,
tumbleweed hair and all.

3

In fact, infant strumpet,
little tramp,
you're looking absolutely fab
running around with nothing on –

except a worried looking pup
with a faceful of creases
sitting on your head
like a hat,

and a little silver triangle
dangling seductively
on a low-slung
black string around your hips

– Oh Ur-Urvashi,
proto Jezebel,
Theda Barra in the bud,
avatara of Mata Hari.

I wish you all the luck.
May the silver flash between your legs
be a beacon
to sailors lost on stormy seas.

All in good time.
But, in the meanwhile,
I wish you would stop tormenting
that poor puppy.

You've worn him like a hat,
walked him like a wheelbarrow,
and played him like
a concertina.

Leave the poor thing alone.
Go chase a crow
for a change;
play hopscotch,

or, better still,
sit
on the thick end of a coconut frond,
and get your brother to drag you around

in real style,
preceded by three hundred leaves,
bowing and scraping,
and singing hosannas in one voice.

Pinwheel

1

A little strip of paper, with
a twist in the middle
and stuck through with a pin,

makes a frail propeller,
no bigger than a dragonfly;
but it begins to spin.

Not all at once.
Halting at first,
a tremor, a twitch,

a pause. Another twitch,
a cautious revolution,
a small hitch.

A sudden counter-revolution
(not bad)
followed by a longish pause

to assimilate the lessons learnt.
But once it understands
its hidden purpose,

it begins to rev up
in real earnest;
and should be able to develop

the thrust required
to lift
the skinny ten-year-old

boy-inventor of the pinwheel who,
bare-arse naked,
has been running around

the traffic island in
crazy circles that, by now, have evolved
into a figure 8 pattern,

pinwheel held
by the tail-end of the pin
in a pinch;

a streamlined arm
extended before him like
a fuselage in the slipstream

of the paper propeller;
shoulder, elbow, wrist,
all beautifully aligned

to the axis of the pin;
and the other arm
raised sideways like a wing.

2

A pi-dog, who thinks of himself
as the original
inhabitant of the island,

watches him
out of a corner of his eye
with increasing unease.

He knows he is looking
at that most dangerous thing on earth,
a young boy with a newfound toy;

and just can't wait for him
to take off –
and smash into the nearest raintree,

come crashing down through the roof
of the principal's house
on top of Elphinstone College,

or, after circling over the city
in an ever-widening spiral,
disappear altogether

into the blue
(sigh!),
in a meteor shower

far too insignificant
for any observatory on earth
to record.

An Old Bicycle Tyre

1

An old bicycle tyre
I may be,
a bald wheel peel,
an endless eel,

a wobbly zero,
a spastic shunya –
but that doesn't mean
I'm ready

to hang myself
up on a finial yet,
or rot
on a mossy rooftop

in the company
of a three-legged chair,
a left shoe grinning
from ear to ear,

and a homeless snail
caught
in the vicious circle
of my cunt.

2

And I'm not about
to join some silly commune
of ascetic
bicycle tyres

that live in colonies
on treetops
and, on no-moon nights,
are said to rise in flocks

to just freewheel,
chase each other from
horizon to horizon,
mate freely,

or play skygames
all night long,
before returning to their perches
on host trees

in the small hours
of the morning,
there to remain
in suspended animation

until the next
no-moon night.
Bunk, if you ask me.
And besides,

I just don't see myself
up there somehow,
on a batty banyan
or a grandiose raintree.

3

I certainly don't intend
to let cicadas piss on me,
bats shit on me,

or a *Tachardia Lacca*
varnish my hide.
No way.
I would immolate myself

and stink up a fine
winter morning
to warm some shivering bums
by the roadside

rather than listen
to a cricket tuning up
his one-inch
electric Stradivarius,

let alone a whole
orchestra of crickets
performing
under the stars

indulging
in pseudo –
Wagnerian excesses,
God forbid.

Certainly
not as long as
there's enough mileage
left in me

to give
a slap-happy boy
a good run
for his money

or enough boys
left in the world
to give me
a good hard slap

on the bottom,
followed by another,
and then another
in quick succession.

I shudder
every time I get a whack,
but that's what keeps me
going, I guess,

what I actually
live for.
And what I want to
know is,

when you're my age,
how many boys
will still be running
after you,

Mam?

Lice

1

She hasn't been a woman for very long,
that girl who looks
like a stick of cinnamon.

Yes, the one in the mustard coloured sari
and red glass bangles,
sitting on that upright concrete block

as if it were a throne,
though it's hardly broad enough
for a kitten to curl up on.

The slender wooden pillar
of the Wayside Inn porch
rises behind her

like some kind of exotic backrest
– how well it seems to fit
the space between her shoulder blades.

2

She has been talking nonstop,
jabbering away like this
and laughing so much all day,

because they let him out of jail this morning
and her dirty no-good lover
is back with her again.

Just look at him, the yob
– the one sitting on the ground
with an arm wrapped around her legs.

She's holding court,
gesticulating from time to time
with her hands like sparrows.

How raptly he's listening to her, that fellow
with a foot on the fender
and an elbow on the bonnet of a parked Fiat.

She has them all spellbound;
but not for one moment has she forgotten
that she has a job on her hands.

3

Her lover's lousy head,
pillowed on her thighs,
has become a harp in her hands.

As her fairy fingers run through his hair,
producing arpeggios of lice
and harmonics of nits,

as bangles softly tinkle over him,
he drifts off and dreams
that he's holed up in a mossy cave

behind a story-telling waterfall
booby-trapped with rainbows,
and hears the distant bark of police dogs.

Kerosene

1

She has always been
the favourite daughter
of that grand old banyan tree

which has started looking youthful
overnight
– with unhappy results, as you can see –

ever since the merry
municipal axemen
went on one of their periodic sprees

yesterday and (sacrilege)
hacked its Yahwist beard
and wild hair;

and she has been sitting
in the reduced but no-less-fatherly-
for-that-reason shade,

playing cards with some of her
friends or sisters
– her maids of honour, one is tempted to say –

and talking about her favourite film stars,
AIDS,
and how much the new cop wants to be paid.

2

She picks a card (Oh good,
the queen of spades),
leaves her highness happily sandwiched

between a jack and a king,
and is wondering which one to discard
– the ace of diamonds or the jack of hearts –

when, unable to make up her mind,
she looks past her cards
for inspiration at the road beyond

and ZOOM
– her eyes come to focus on
a passing kerosene cart.

3

She folds her cards like a Japanese fan,
puts them down beside her
on the ground,

and is up in a flash.
She grabs an empty plastic jerrycan
from among her things (Oh, odds and ends:

cardboard cartons, pots and pans,
bundles of cloth, a beheaded doll, a small
transistor, a beachball on a Primus stove)

that surround the girth of the banyan
and sprout on its trunk
like some exotic parasitic growth

– and she's off.
She has had one in the oven
for about seven months by the look of things,

but she is still in her teens,
the pregnant queen of tarts,
and she can still run like a gazelle when she wants.

4

Sari pulled up to her knees
and jerrycan in hand she runs,
shanks flashing,

with the loping stride of, well,
a gazelle, a lame one perhaps,
but a gazelle none the less.

A scooter spins around,
a white Mercedes stops to let her pass
as she cuts across the street

blind to everything else,
to head off the kerosene cart
before it disappears round the bend.

5

Perhaps he knows her;
that young buck pulling the cart,
the shirtless klutz,

the jogger between the shafts,
sweat glistening
on his black athletic back,

pantlegs rolled up to his calves.
For, on seeing her, he stops;
says something to her. She laughs.

The cart tilts forward when he bends
to set the front ends of its shafts
on the ground.

A bit of a clown, he pirouettes
on one foot,
steps over the crosstie,

bows to the lady, and asks her
to follow him to the back of the cart,
with an airy wave of his hand.

6

The cartwheel with its many
sturdy wooden spokes
offers him a choice of sensible footholds.

He disdains them all;
refuses the legup
promised by the solid-looking hub.

An elegant leap takes him to the top
of one of the short ends of the shafts
that jut out at the back

beyond the buckboard,
and he starts jumping up and down on it
with all his might

and both his feet,
like a chimp in heat,
until the cart rears,

seesaws uncertainly
on its axletree, and
finally, tips backwards,

tilting the balance in favour
of the tap
located at the back of the cask.

7

After they have gone – he
with his cart
to complete his rounds of deliveries,

she with her jerrycan, now full,
to deposit it between
the buttresses of the banyan

and to pick up her cards,
her mind made up
to discard the jack of hearts –

an old crow lands on the edge
of a small puddle of kerosene
left on the road,

shakes his head,
declares it unfit for corvine consumption
and flies off in disgust

to perch on the steeple
of St Andrew's church,
from where he sees a sight

that never fails to cheer him up:
the butcher about to enter Lion Gate
on his bicycle

with the daily supply
of meat
for the dockyard canteen.

Knucklebones

1

Hand on hip you sit, straightbacked
in a torchwood yellow sari, blouse ditto,
playing knucklebones with some of your friends

on the pavement; a bright red plastic haircomb
stuck at a rakish angle just above
the helix of your ear, in centre-parted

raven hair tightly coiled into a bun
that stays well above the hairline
and does not allow even strays to spoil

the clean line of your high and haughty neck
– dark as the lowgrade hash you sell,
and a seemingly endless supply of which

you can produce at will, by reaching down
into the depths of your well-stocked cleavage,
guarded at all times by two alert breasts.

114

2

Your legs are a matched pair of clasp-knives;
the left one folded in at the knee,
and the right one that, blade out, shows its steel.

Lawyers, bankers, painters, shop assistants –
everyone passing by – can set his watch
according to your legs (it's ten past ten).

The space between your legs is a playing field;
and your right hand a mad myna that keeps
hopping about in it, pecking at pebbles.

3

Every time you throw the seven pebbles,
a new constellation is formed between
the longitudes of your wideangle legs,

but this time you goofed, admit it, my dear;
you've gone and got yourself the Little Bear
– and now you're going to be in big trouble.

No. The way those pebbles have scattered may
pose a problem to any other player,
but I guess you are a born bear-slayer.

You pick up the North Star and toss it up.
Sweep up the remaining six off the ground
in the time it takes – no more than a sec –

for it to come down like a falling star
in the hollow of your hand, with a click,
to meet its mates already nestling there.

Someone comes along and asks for a pill
– an Elphinstone boy, by the looks of him –
and oh oh oh your foot's got pins and needles.

4

You get up with a big smile on your bum.
Your sari wears a grin
where your buttocks have sucked it in.

Which sets us all back by a good ten seconds.
It isn't just your sari;
it's time itself that feels the pinch.

The clock outside the Lund & Blockley shop
that shows the different times
in all the big cities around the globe

stumbles and loses ten seconds worldwide.
Flights are delayed.
Trains run behind schedule.

India's new experimental rocket
stands in a daze, after the blastoff,
and blows up on the launch pad.

The governor and the foundation stone
of a new petrochemical complex
both get laid in the general confusion.

But you show great presence of mind,
and take corrective measures
before something really terrible happens.

Time unpuckers when you smooth your behind.
The earth resumes its normal rate of spin.
No harm done.

Ten lost seconds may not leave
a permanent scar on eternity.
But these things tend to add up, you know,

and postpone the apocalypse
or bypass it altogether. Well!
Don't do it again's all I can say.

To a Charas Pill

Little devil,
did you grow up on a farm
on the shadowy slopes of distant Afghanistan?

Did you have a rough ride
in a pickup truck
as you bounced along in a cloud of dust,

down muletracks and winding dirt roads?
Or did you cross the Khyber Pass on a camel's back
in the company of brigands?

You've come a long way;
travelled a thousand miles;
crossed many rivers and deserts;

got past many fences, checkpoints, borders and boundaries.
But all that's behind you, baby,
and now your troubles are over.

You've come to a place
where you're completely safe,
where you feel like you were back home again.

Here rest,
and be refreshed
between my breasts,

until I tell you
to come out of hiding
and do what you came here to do:

first caress,
then fuck up
a good man's mind.

Go, you little devil.
Bury him alive,
bury the whole lot of them.

Like a landslide in the Hindu Kush can
bury a whole army
of ten thousand horsemen.

And remember.
The blessings of my breasts
go with you.

A Game of Tigers and Sheep

Who has the tigers and who the sheep
never seems to make any difference.
The result is always the same:
she wins,
I lose.

But sometimes when her tigers
are on the rampage,
and I've lost half my herd of sheep,
help comes from unexpected quarters:
above.

The rusty shield-bearer,
neutral till then,
paradrops a winning flower
– yellow
and irrelevant –

on the checkerboard
drawn on the pavement in charcoal,
cutting off the retreat
of one tiger,
and giving a check to the other;

and quickly follows it up
with another flower
– just as yellow
and just as irrelevant – except
that it comes down even more slowly;

a flower without a search warrant
that brushes past her earlobe,
grazes her cheek,
and disappears down the front
of her low-cut blouse

– where she usually keeps
her stash of hash –
to confuse her even further, with its mildly
narcotic
but very distracting fragrance.

The Barefoot Queen of the Crossroads

1

She is dark as bitter chocolate,
the witch of Rampart Row,
the barefoot queen of the crossroads.

She has dominion
over two traffic islands
and three pavements.

She has the larger traffic island
all to herself at the moment,
if you don't count the dogs.

Her title to the island is contested
only by a trespassing sunbeam
– just a wedge

that has grown
very fast into a corridor of light
that cuts the island in two.

But she's not standing in its path
to challenge it,
or contest its right of way.

She has washed her hair this morning
and she's standing with her back to the sun
to dry it

and the huge damp patch
on her clean white
but slightly rumpled petticoat,

which is what she's wearing at the moment,
apart from a yellow choli above
and silver anklets below

playing hide and seek
in the scalloped shadow of her petticoat.
She has yet to wear her sari.

That damp patch is about the size of China;
but its borders that stretch
from her buttocks in the north

to the bend of her knees
in the south
are rapidly shrinking in the sun.

2

She whirls around, with a start almost,
as if the sun
had slapped her on her bottom - hard.

Her eyes close;
the sun explodes
and goes nova behind her lids.

The sun covers her face with kisses.
It flutters
like a hummingbird before her navel

and drinks up
a sparkling drop of water
like nectar from a buttercup.

She throws her head forward
to bring her hair from back to front;
all of her hair, in one black mass

leaps upwards into the air,
to come surging forward and fall
in front of her face like a black torrent.

Legs spread apart,
bare feet planted firmly on the ground,
she bends forward at the waist.

She stands there swaying from side to side,
shaking her head, rhythmically,
like a cow elephant in a trance.

She threshes her hair with downward strokes,
with the midsection
of a chunky towel, twisted over twice

and held taut between two hands
at both ends,
in what could be called a Nanchaku grip.

She scatters spitfire droplets of water
all around her;
they dart about like rainbow-tailed moths.

Then she straightens up
and, with a single toss of her head,
she sends her hair flying back again

– in one body,
like a well-trained circus animal
at the crack of a whip.

And then, wrapped around
and rolled up nicely in her towel,
untwisted now,

she piles up her hair
on top of her head in tight coils,
like a great white conch.

3

One end of her sari
(red like the city in May,
with all its gulmohurs in bloom),

say the downtown end,
wrapped around the petticoat, damp no more,
and secured at the hips;

and the uptown end arranged
over the left shoulder
and left dangling behind,

she holds the sari away from her
at arm's length
at a halfway point along the border,

from where it's a short walk
to the belly
for her three fingers and thumb,

as they collect the sari
along the way
in neat accordion folds

(flip flap, flip flap,
Dadar, Parel, Lalbaug, Byculla, Bori Bunder,
flip flap, Flora Fountain

and flip, we come to Kala Ghoda,
which is where
we've been, all along),

and tuck it in at the waist
about three inches below the navel
– which winks

as she sucks her stomach in
and out,
to airlock the sari in place.

4

She might as well be
at some place like the Queen's Step-well
in Patan,

or a courtyard in Alhambra,
surrounded by eunuchs
in 13th-century Granada,

for all she seems to care;
screened as she seems to be by
utter contempt

for the voyeur world revolving
around her
– the dirty old men with clean noses,

the bug-eyed painters,
poets with their tongues hanging out,
and other jerks and assorted arseholes.

And if that Peeping Tom,
with the rabbinical beard
and a Persian potentate's turban,

sticking his head out of a hole
above the library archway
wants to ogle,

she neither knows
nor cares.
It's no skin off her nose

or shin.

Breakfast Time at Kala Ghoda

1

The clock displayed outside
the Lund & Blockley shop across the road
is the big daddy of all clocks,

and will correct me if I'm wrong;
but I think it's tonight already
in Tokyo,

where they're busy polishing off
sliced raw fish,
sushi balls and tofu with soy sauce;

and the emperor's chopsticks are poised,
at this very moment,
over Hatcho Miso, his favourite dish.

In a restaurant in Seoul,
a dog is slowly being strangled
before it's thrown into a cooking pot.

2

It's still last night in the Americas.
In the state penitentiary of Texas,
a condemned man is tucking into

a T-bone steak, two cheeseburgers, french fries,
a tossed salad with thousand island dressing
and four cartons of milk.

Juliana Quispe is cooking potatoes
over llama dung fire
in her stone house in southern Peru.

Someone's hanging freshly butchered
reindeer meat
in his smokehouse in Alaska.

And aboard Salyut, the Russian spaceship,
the cosmonauts have just finished their breakfast
of pork, cheese, honeycake, prunes and coffee.

3

Leja dreams it's raining bread.
She's a child again.
She runs out in the streets to look up,

the streets of Gora Kalvaria,
where she grew up.
The sky is full of angels in dive bombers.

The loaves explode as soon as they land.
A loaf lands
on her father's bread factory.

It blows up.
The shock hurls her to the ground.
She wakes up in her bed,

unable to recognise her own
one-room apartment in Baniocha, near Warsaw,
where she's the only Jew left.

She stares at the matzos on the table,
freckled
like her own 90-year-old skin,

and wonders where they came from;
and what happened
to everybody.

4

After giving suck
unsuccessfully
to her newborn baby

that she has brought
into the world
with no help from anyone

– cutting the birthstring
with a flintknife,
cleaning up afterwards –

doing it all by herself
like any other
Gola woman,

like her own mother
before her,
and her mother before her,

fifteen-year-old
Nagamma,
on her hands and knees,

has come out of
the opening
of her gudulu

– more an upside-down nest
made up of leaves
than a birthing hut,

just large enough
to contain
a mother and her child –

and is crawling
on all fours,
in the direction of

two idlis
placed on a jackfruit leaf
twenty feet away

that she intends to convert
into milk
for her child

– a miracle
she alone
can perform.

5

In Bandagere
in Andhra Pradesh,
or may be somewhere else in India,

thirteen high-caste Hindus
are forcing four dalits to eat
human excreta,

which is to say
shit,
right now,

for letting their cattle graze
in the jowar fields
of an upper-caste landlord, say,

if not for
some other
reason.

6

Nearer home, in Bombay itself,
the miserable bunch
of drunks, delinquents, smalltime crooks

and the usual suspects
have already been served their morning kanji
in Byculla jail.

They've been herded together now
and subjected
to an hour of force-fed education.

One unfortunate wretch
has been made to stand, book in hand,
in front of a captive audience

interested more in horseplay,
fisticuffs and insider trading
in cigarettes and charas pills

than in listening to a one-page biography
of Jawaharlal Nehru
in a tattered highschool text book.

All attempts the reader makes
to decipher the text before him
and string syllables into words

(Ja Ja Ja Ja Wa Wa Ja wa Huh Huh Huh Huh Ruh
Ja wahar La La Lala)
get lost among the more fluent Ma Chudaos

and other obscenities, until
the class is not so much as dismissed – it collapses
as soon as the morning inspection is over.

7

They're serving khima pao at Olympia,
dal gosht at Baghdadi,
puri bhaji at Kailash Parbat,

aab gosht at Sarvi's,
kebabs with sprigs of mint at Gulshan-e-Iran,
nali nehari at Noor Mohamadi's,

baida ghotala at the Oriental,
paya soup at Benazir,
brun maska at Military Café,

upma at Swagat,
shira at Anand Vihar,
and fried eggs and bacon at Wayside Inn.

For, yes, it's breakfast time at Kala Ghoda
as elsewhere
in and around Bombay

– up and down
the whole hungry longitude, in fact;
the 73rd, if I'm not mistaken.

8

Look:
The lady with a head of wirewool hair,
peppercorn eyes,

and a motherly smile for everyone
is here already,
carrying

a jumbo aluminium box full of idlis
– lying
like an infant Krishna,

roly-poly,
and rocking gently on a bed of
almond leaves

inside a basket
balanced on her head,
and a bucket full of sambar,

fit for fire-eaters,
in her hand.
Where is everybody?

9

Not to worry.
For it's breakfast time at Kala Ghoda,
and they'll all be here.

Let Our Lady of Idlis
(I call her Annapoorna)
set her basket down.

Don't just stand there
– help the lady with the basket, man;
where's your manners!

Let her settle down nicely
on one of those
low concrete blocks that skirt the lesser island

(appended like Serendip
to the much larger one, which is almost
subcontinental in proportion).

She'll choose the third block along the base
of the isosceles,
counting from the Wayside Inn end –

you'll see.
What did I tell you?
That's her favourite seat.

Now, let her arrange her things
around herself,
the way she wants them,

and the whole gang will be here
the moment she's ready
to start dishing out idlis on almond leaves

and ladling out sambar,
directly down your throat if you like,
unless you've brought your

mug along.
I told you to,
didn't I?

10

A kitten cradled
in the crook of his arm
and a yellow dog

at his feet,
the blind man is sitting
sideways on his cot

with the music shop
behind him,
and talking to grandma

seated nearby
on the pavement,
behind the little vamp

and trying, comb in hand,
to make some sense
of the little one's hair.

11

The yellow dog
at the blind man's feet,
who has been following the progress

of a small group of Jews
– returning from the synagogue
in Rope Walk Lane

to their homes in Colaba
presumably –
with a singular lack of interest,

suddenly comes to life
when he sees
a familiar figure emerge

through a gap in the wall of
Jewish backs,
is up on his feet and wagging his tail.

12

The little vamp cries,
'Idlis',
and slips out of grandma's hands.

Grandma sends the comb
flying after the girl
and then decides

to follow in the footsteps
of her granddaughter.
Time for idlis, she says

to herself, as well as
for the blind man's benefit,
and rises to her feet.

A major production, that.
Have you ever seen
an old elephant do that?

13

Lovingly, the blind man
strokes
his vaguely military-looking moustache

with divide-and-rule fingers;
caresses
both the twirled ends,

forever jealous of each other,
by turns,
giving equal attention to both;

instructs
every hair to keep out of the way,
when idlis are in transit;

and reaches
for his shoulder-high stick
lying on the cot within easy reach.

The kitten jumps off his forearm,
slips down a gap
in the criss-cross ropes of the cot,

tries to hang on to the rope
with its nails,
before dropping to the ground.

From where it sees the blind man
head for the idlis,
tap-tapping the road ahead with his stick,

the yellow dog running ahead of him
and barking
to give him his bearings.

Not to be left out,
the kitten
runs after him.

   14
The tight lid
of the jumbo aluminium box
opens

with the collective
sigh
of a hundred idlis

waiting to exhale,
followed
by a rush to the exit

– a landslide of fullmoons
slithering
past each other,

to tumble in a jumble,
and pile up
in a shallow basket,

an orgy,
a palpitating hill
of naked idlis

slipping and sliding
clambering over
and suffocating each other.

   15
The little vamp, the grandma, the blind man,
the ogress,
the rat-poison man,

the pinwheel boy,
the hipster queen of the crossroads,
the Demosthenes of Kala Ghoda,

the pregnant queen of tarts,
the laughing Buddha,
the knucklebones champ –

the island slowly begins to fill up.
Not just with the children
and the grandchildren of the banyan

and their cats and dogs,
but with all their friends and cousins as well,
from near and far.

16

Each and every hungry and homeless soul
within a mile of the little island
is soon gravitating towards it

to receive the sacrament of idli,
to anoint palates
with sambar,

to celebrate anew, every morning,
the seduction and death
of the demon of hunger

(threatening the entire world)
at the hands of Gauri
in the form of a humble idli.

They come from all over;
walking, running, dancing, limping, stumbling, rolling
– each at his own speed.

17

Where's the laughing Buddha?
Oh, there she is,
sambar drooling down her chin;

the laughing (and sometimes giggling) Buddha,
born again
in a turnip-headed woman's body,

benevolent blubber mostly;
who never gets
involved in an argument with a sari,

and wisely goes about
wrapped in what looks suspiciously like a bedsheet
and a baggy choli.

18

Why, the old pirate's here too
– a bandannaed head
bobbing over a turbulent beard white as foam,

and a pegleg painted a deep crimson –
trying to pass himself off as an ordinary beggar
with a mug in his hand.

19

And here comes the shoeshine boy
– he really fancies himself
as the funkiest kid on the block, doesn't he? –

in a black tanktop,
the bottoms of his black pants rolled up to his knees,
and swinging his shoe-rest

– not only his mobile shop,
but his practice drum as well,
painted a cheerful red and yellow.

Hasn't lost a minute either
to start flirting with the girls,
has he?

20

And he must really be hungry,
that old paralytic in a wheelchair
made by cannibalising two bicycles,

cranking a relocated pedal with one hand,
and honking away
on an old car-horn with the other

– a real antique that horn, red bulb and all –
tied to the handlebar with a stout piece of string,
to announce his arrival.

21

Ah, but here comes the legless hunchback
to beat him to it
and win by several lengths.

And nobody's surprised;
for the speed-king of Bombay comes zipping
and hurtling along as usual,

riding his homemade skateboard
of rude wood
hammered together by a friendly carpenter;

weaving in and out of traffic,
cutting across lanes, jumping signals,
and flying over speedbreakers;

pushing the road back, expertly,
with his bare hands,
and with a big grin on his face.

22

Bowls, katoras, mugs
and assorted receptacles
come forward.

Idlis pair off,
extricate themselves
from the promiscuous heap

first chance they get,
and the moment they find themselves
alone together,

lie gasping,
belly to belly,
or hump each other

like turtles
in the mating season
– wherever you look,

in bowls, mugs, katoras,
in plates,
on almond leaves.

Only to be swamped
by tidal waves
of sambar.

23

Islands of idlis float
belly up
or splash about

in seas of sambar,
among the wreckage
of red chilli peppers,

submerged aubergines,
torpedoed tomatoes,
peppercorn mines,

drumsticks
drifting
like shattered masts.

Or, like oil-slick
seals,
blink in the sun.

24

Idlis,
plump and spongy lenses,
magnify our appetites;

and, through the telescope
of shared hope,
bring the stars within our reach.

25

Sitting in a corner of the island,
clutching
a bowl to his bosom,

legs stretched out before him,
and elbows resting
on two sides of the triangle,

the laidback leper's looking as comfortable
as if he were
in the bow of a dugout,

drifting lazily towards
the healing shores of a continent
where he will be whole again;

every green bump of his cleanshaven
and well-oiled head
glistening to God's glory,

as the sun palpates him
like a phrenologist
to study the contours of his cranium;

twenty blind eyelets staring back
from a pair of laceless tennis shoes
at his nose-holes.

26

And who's that scruffy looking stranger
with dirty yellow hair
sleeping with his head pillowed on a concrete block?

A bird of passage,
a hippy
who spent last night on this island.

We've never seen him before, have we?
Is he alive?
Is he asleep?

What country you come from, Sir?
You got dollars? Pounds? Oh, never mind!
You hungry?

Here.
You can try some of this stuff
from my plate.

Good?
You like?
Good!

27

Boy, am I glad they've left
at least
this one tiny traffic island alone;

haven't landscaped it to death,
put a fence around it,
and slapped logos all over it.

So why don't you take your bowl of idlis
and find yourself
somewhere to sit down like everybody else?

Aren't these blocks of concrete wonderful?
Let's not forget to thank
whoever it was that invented them.

A most useful piece of street furniture,
I must say.
Make great road dividers,

great traffic-island markers
and, more to the point, great settees.
By the way,

they make great pillows too,
in case you feel like a snooze afterwards
and if you like them hard, the way I do.

28

The smell of food alone,
by itself,
does not make an injured rat,

its back broken in three places,
leave
the safety of its hole

– built cunningly
under the protective root
of a mahogany –

not unless
it's starving as well,
and has to come out in the open

in broad daylight,
hoping no one will notice.
But someone does.

Always.
Shit.
A little boy

who sees in it
an opportunity of getting
some batting practice,

not to be missed.
He goes and gets his cricket bat
from behind

a jerrycan of kerosene,
comes forward
to take his position at the crease,

puts his weight on the front foot,
and hits the rat
with the meat of his bat.

He's going for his shots,
with his hysterical kid-sister
screaming for blood.

He has brought the bat up
to drive the rat
to the extra-cover boundary,

when his mother
takes it right out of his hands
(is that cricket?),

lifts the naked batsman,
the young master,
up in her arms,

brings him back to the
pavilion
to put some clothes on him

and, his legs flying in the air,
takes him to the little traffic island
to feed him.

Like all good mothers, she knows
that good breakfasts
make good cricketers.

29

A delegation of crows
from the neighbourhood,
including some

from the raintrees
and the mountain ebonies
around the Museum,

and augmented by
opportunists
from further afield

– like the wild almond
in the University garden,
the star-apples

around Flora Fountain,
the jamun tree
near the Bhika Behram well –

are quick to arrive
on the scene,
as usual.

They camp
in the middle of the road,
waving black flags;

scatter
to let a car pass,
and reform,

all their beaks,
like magnetic needles,
pointing in one direction.

30

The convergence
of all the loose appetite in the air
within a one-mile radius

to that one spot
has created a bubble in time,
shimmering with the joy of living,

reflecting all the colours
of hope,
and about forty-five minutes across.

It lasts
for as long as Annapoorna is there,
and a little longer.

A sort of an after-image, a glow,
lingers behind
for a while after she packs up and leaves,

with a lighter basket on her head,
an empty bucket in her hand,
and a full purse at her waist.

31

The pop-up cafeteria
disappears
like a castle in a children's book

– along with the king and the queen,
the courtiers,
the court jester and the banqueting hall,

the roast pheasants and the suckling pigs,
as soon as the witch
shuts the book on herself –

and the island returns
to its flat old
boring self.

Words for a Cellist

The music class is over.
His fiddler friends have gone
their separate ways

with all their fiddles
and fiddlesticks,
leaving him alone

with his awkward burden
beside him on the pavement
in front of Max Mueller Bhavan

with no taxi in sight,
clenching and unclenching his hands,
cursing Purcell,

Boccherini, Beethoven,
watching the beggars' banquet,
and letting

the philharmonic gulmohur
speckle him
and the cello lying at his feet

in its contoured coffin
like a stillborn elephant,
with leaves

that keep falling
like yellow
– and slightly elongated – minims,

in a deciduous symphony.

The Shit Sermon

1

When the drunk
– who has slept through it all
and, consequently,

missed out on the action,
as well as his proteins –
wakes,

he finds himself marooned,
all alone,
shirtless and hungry,

on a tiny deserted island,
hugging
an empty bottle to his bosom.

He puts it away thoughtfully
in the space
between two concrete blocks,

with the vague idea
that it may come in handy
to send

a message in a bottle
to the world
at large

– should he so decide
at some point of time
in the future.

2

He gets up
and examines the island
bounded on three sides.

He paces the isosceles,
measuring the sides,
the median and the altitude,

muttering
and talking to himself the while,
like a dingbat Demosthenes

practising oratory,
pebbles in mouth,
on the seashore.

He stands facing east,
at the easternmost point
of the island,

and blinks uncomprehendingly
at the sun,
through a haze of rum,

wondering
where he has seen it before.
He decides

that it's not
the missing top button
of his grungy green pants.

3

He rubs his nose,
and delivers his first Philippic
against the sun

– a diatribe
against the great arsehole
in the sky.

He turns around in disgust.
He pulls at an earlobe,
scratches his beard.

God is great, he says.
He has given all his creatures,
great and small,

two holes:
a feedhole and a shithole,
and He will provide.

Usne sabko diyela hai
– khaneko muh,
hugneko gaand.

God is great, he says,
shouting.
I shall not want.

4

He adjusts the folds
of the soft December morning
around him like a himation.

He yawns and stretches.
A crackling corona
blazes around his dusty hair.

He thrusts a barbed beard
at the fossilised
upstart from Baghdad

with his talmudic beard,
looking down on him
from above the library arch,

and spits on him
– working up
a good spitball in his mouth.

5

Shit city, he thunders;
the lion of Bombay thunders,
Shit City!

I shit on you.
You were a group
of seven shitty islands

given in dowry
to the Shit King of Ing
to shit on

– and now it's all
one big high-rise shit,
waiting for God

to pull the flush.
And it won't be long.
For God is great.

The words rise
like a flock of shadow ravens
from his mouth,

circle in the sky above,
over the stock exchange,
the High Court and Mantralaya,

before settling down
on the rooftops
all around.

A pi-dog sneaks up on him
from behind
and bites him on the arse.

Watermelons

1

All the clocks along the way
stop
to let the watermelon cart pass.

The city holds its breath
as the cart goes click-clack,
prolonging the road,

stretching the morning
to eternity;
finding potholes where there are none;

sides splitting with watermelons
packed like felons
on their way to the gallows;

led by a dappled Konkani bull,
compact as they come
(a regular young Trotsky,

if someone who likes to trot
can be described as such),
with pink pompoms on bloodred horns

and bells around the dewlap
that mingle their jingle-jangle
with the general slap-bang and clatter.

2

On a ridgepole
that juts out from under the tilt
and doubles as a clothesline,

a skyblue petticoat
flutters
and flirts with the wind,

calling one and all,
young and old, women and children,
to gather round the banner.

A bellyful of hay,
stuffed in a lowslung hammock
below the buckboard,

leaves a trail of straw,
all along the way
from Kalamboli to Colaba

– a travelogue
in shorthand,
punctuated by bullshit.

3

Jumping lynchpins
(hic)
hit the hiccuping axle-ends

hard on the downbeat
at every halfturn of the wheels,
and every time

a wheel discovers a pothole,
it sends a shockwave
through the hill of watermelons.

And though they all look
as cool
as chilled cannonballs,

every shell-shocked watermelon
is held in its place
only by its just-as-shaken neighbours

– a fraternity of frightened
fellow-melons
dreaming of blood, sweat and syrup.

151

But they're truly alarmed
when the cart stops
and all movement ceases.

The seeds stiffen,
each imprisoned in crimson flesh,
in a cavity of its own,

like clusters
of black exclamation points
radiating

from a common centre
!
of anxiety.

4

My heart leaps up
when I behold
a watermelon cart pass by.

The stick drops from my hand.
The bicycle tyre
spins around and flops to the ground,

forgotten already.
Watermelons, I hear a shout,
though no one has actually shouted.

I look around for grandma,
Where's she?
She just loves these Sugarbabies.

But my mum,
she's there already,
walking beside the cart.

Bargaining.
She's good at it.
The cart stops.

I reach there just in time
to see a knife thrust
and a sun burst.

My throat
goes dry.

The Boomtown Lepers' Band

Trrrap a boom chaka
shh chaka boom tap

Ladies and gentlemen (crash),
here comes (bang), here comes (boom)
here comes the Boomtown Lepers' Band,
drumsticks and maracas tied to their hands
bandaged in silk and the finest of gauze,
and clutching tambourines in scaly paws.

Trrrap a boom chaka
shh chaka boom trap

Whack.
Let the city see its lion face
in the flaky mirror of our flesh.
Slap a tambourine (thwack),
let cymbals clash.
Come on, let the coins shake rattle and roll
in our battered aluminium bowl –
as our noseless singer
lets out a half-hearted howl
to belt out a tuneless song
for a city without soul.

Here we come (bang)
and there we go (boom)
pushing the singer in a wheelbarrow.

Trrap a boom chaka
shh chaka boom tap
Trrap a boom chaka
shh chaka boom trapp

Bon Appétit

1

I wish bon appétit
to the frail old fisherwoman

(tiny,
she is no more than just

an armload of bones
grown weightless over the years,

and caught
in a net of wrinkles)

who, on her way to the market,
has stopped

to have a quick breakfast
in a hole-in-the-wall teashop,

and is sitting hunched
over a plate of peas

– her favourite dish –
on a shaky table,

tearing a piece of bread
with her sharp claws

to soak it in the thin gravy
flecked with red chilli peppers;

and whose mouth is watering
at this very moment, I bet,

for I can almost taste
her saliva

in my mouth.

2

And I wish bon appetit
to that scrawny little

motheaten kitten
– so famished it can barely stand,

stringy tail,
bald patch on grungy back,

white skin showing
through sparse fur –

that has emerged
from a small pile of rubbish nearby,

slipped once
on a bit of onion skin,

and, making its way
slowly but unerringly

towards the shallow basket
full of shrimps

that the fisherwoman has left
on the pavement

before entering the teashop,
has finally managed to get there,

raised itself on its hindlegs
to put its dirty paws

on the edge of the basket,
and kissed

its first shrimp.

A Blind Man Strings a Cot

1

His ropedancing fingers fly
diagonally
crisscrossing a rectangular void,

making connections between
the adjacent sides
with a rolling hitch,

joining north to west,
west to south,
bamboo to bamboo.

2

An outline is all he has;
just the bare bones
of a narrow unstrung bed;

the ends of its bamboo sides
whittled crudely
with an adze and fitted

into jackwood legs;
but it's a bed he knows as well
as he knows his own body.

3

The restless bed
tosses and turns in his arms;
he wrestles with it.

The bed puts its front paws
on his shoulders,
and all but starts licking his face.

It stands before him, swaying,
like a drunken doorway,
daring him to walk through,

but he takes it in his arms instead
and starts giving it
dancing lessons.

   4

A big bumbling ball
(bumpety bump)
of kinky coir rope

keeps getting smaller and smaller
as it plays hopscotch
on the pavement.

Oh O O o o it's nothing really;
just a hopalong nothing
on a very long leash.

What makes it so nervous
and gives it a prickly sensation
is the feeling

that it's being constantly watched,
spied upon
by the blind man's familiar.

   5

And, indeed, a velvety cat,
black enough
to have strayed into daylight

straight out of the blind man's
blindworld,
and which could, of course, be reporting to him,

is sitting quietly under a Toyota
parked by the kerbside,
on the inside of the right front wheel,

looking with its golden eyes
from under the fender, unblinkingly,
at the jittery coir ball

and its unravelling.

The Potato Peelers

1

Backlit by their dreams,
they sit on three upended wooden crates,

outside the entrance of a garage
converted into a restaurant kitchen;

elbows on knees,
barechested above their shorts,

hunched over potatoes
rotating slowly in their hands,

and the dark side of each one's mind
faintly visible in

the reflected light
of the others' unspoken thoughts.

2

The three-sided silence
of the potato peelers makes

a prism that seizes on
a fleeting thought that crosses

the mind of a bakery boy
as he parks his bicycle

(staggering under loads of bread,
two monster canvas bags

on either side of the handlebar,
and a third one on the carrier),

and sends a freakish sliver
of an illicit rainbow streaking across,

to touch the mind of a half-witted woman
who looks a bit like a laughing Buddha

and who is still asleep under
the bearded banyan

on a flattened two-ply corrugated paper box,
her clean-shaven head pillowed on a yellow dog,

partly covered by the fragment
of an old cinema poster,

and laughing even in her sleep.

The Rat-poison Man's Lunch Hour

1

The rat-poison man has left
his one-legged poster leaning

against the wall of Wayside Inn
and settled down for lunch on the pavement,

with his back to the poster,
in the polyphonic shade of the banyan.

The dejected poster stands
facing the wall as if it has been punished,

hiding its real thoughts
and showing its blank,

unsized and uncommunicative side
to passers-by.

An expressionless oblong of white canvas
stretched on a wooden frame,

with a wooden bar that divides it
vertically in two equal halves

and continues past the base
to form a short stumpy leg

with a chunky three-inch wheel
grafted onto its club-foot,

the whole construct designed
never to challenge

the average Indian male
vertically.

2

The poster shows a dozen rats
emblazoned on an azure field.

Some dead, some dying,
in various stages of agony.

Black, brown and grey rats.
One a rare blue at dexter base.

Some have tails like corkscrews,
some like unrepentant awls.

At peace at last
with their incisors

(or do they keep growing
even after death?),

their whiskers are sharp
like poison-tipped needles,

and they all seem to glow
with an electric blue aura,

a kind of
radioactive nirvana.

3

Foreheads touching,
they exchange paranoias,

share anxieties, confidences, histories, hopes
– with a total lack of comprehension.

With its peeling paint and plaster,
the wall offers what consolation it can,

but it fails to understand
the hate-filled world of the rat-poison poster,

its obsession with death
– the only truth it seems to know -

its vision
of the final battle between good and evil,

fought bitterly in two dimensions,
with cheap enamel paint and biological weapons,

with a clearly defined enemy
and a clear plan of action.

4

The wall can talk about an old hat shop
that doesn't even exist any more.

It can talk about cheerful red-checked tablecloths,
blue Delftware and rose windows,

cut-glass vinegar bottles with round stoppers
and antique silver-plated cruet stands.

Boy meets Girl at the Corner Table
is a story it never tires of telling,

and remembers all the old songs from the thirties onwards
– from Saigal and Bessie Smith to Guns and Roses –

as new ones keep percolating from the music shop next door
and creating new neural pathways in its cement.

It remembers Babasaheb sitting all by himself
with a pot of tea and scribbling notes,

dreaming with an audacious pencil
of a society undivided by caste and creed.

It remembers an obscure poet munching on Welsh rabbit,
and thinking of rats dying in a wet barrel.

That's the only bit the poster understands,
dismissing everything else

as so much bullshit mousse and sentimental custard.
It even suspects that the wall,

spongy with nostalgia,
may actually have a soft corner for rats.

   5

A lawyer walks into Wayside Inn
softly humming 'Aasamaa pe hai khuda',

is glad to see that his favourite table
is empty, orders a beer, takes a sip

and, licking the foam off his upper lip
contentedly, leans back in his chair,

which brings the bald patch on his occiput
in direct contact with the exact spot

on the inner side of the wall
that's in touch with the rat-poison poster.

The wall's good enough to provide him with
the words to the second line of the song

that he has been trying to remember all day;
and the poison poster's only too happy

to secretly plant the seed of a deathwish
in the lawyer's head without his knowledge

– a seed that will take its own good time
to germinate, but germinate it will.

6

A dismissive flick of his little finger
slices the top off a hill of rice.

A few quick jabs of fingertips,
and a crater opens before him.

The woman in a plain red nylon sari,
choli to match and hibiscus in hair,

dips a ladle in an aluminium vessel
that sits with a sooty bottom on a Primus stove,

and tips it over the steaming crater.
The hill collapses on itself,

volcanic sambar starts oozing out
of fissures that open in its south face.

*

Whoever he is – her husband, pimp, cousin –
the woman has a lot to say to him,

for she has been doing all the talking,
as the two of them sit under the banyan

on the opposite sides of the same thali,
and he has been nodding from time to time,

mechanically, as he sends volley
after volley of fire-and-forget riceballs

in the general direction of his face,
without cease or let.

*

A riceball leaves, or rather, slips out of his hand,
as soon as his fingers have formed it;

it gathers speed as it rises,
gets past the defences of his beard,

blasts a gaping hole in his face
– even before it can be hit –

to burst in his mouth
and to zap him on his palate.

*

As more and more rice
is transferred to his belly,

the thali, too, begins
to nod along with him;

imperceptibly at first,
and then quite vigourously

– in unconscious imitation of the man,
perhaps, or may be because, by now,

the thali, too, has really got involved
in what the woman has to say,

or may be because the steadying influence
of the rice is fast disappearing

until, towards the end of the meal,
it rocks so violently

that the man has to hold it down,
physically, with one hand,

so that he can make
a clean sweep of it with the other.

*

The woman pours some water from a mug
for the man to wash his hands in the thali,

which produces a passable drum solo,
to act as a coda to one man's lunch.

They both get up; he says something to her,
pats her affectionately on the bottom

as she bends to pick up the sloppy thali
and he turns away to reclaim his poster;

and holding it before him like a shield,
is ready, once again, to face the world,

happy, once again, as who wouldn't be,
with a singular truth to hide behind.

David Sassoon

1

I, who in my day
was known as the merchant prince
of Bombay

and lived like a Persian potentate
in this city
that I had no mean share in building,

am stuck like a schmuck up here
– an ahmaq,
a certified keer-e-khar –

sticking my pilloried head
out of a medallion
in the pediment above the archway

of the Mechanics Institute
– sorry, I mean
the library that bears my name –

my nose pointing towards Lion Gate,
my beard pointing straight down
to the dogshit (or worse) by the kerbside,

my soul in Sheol,
my bones in a grave somewhere on the grounds
of a synagogue in Poona.

2

Oh, that's no sweat,
not having a body, I mean;
most of the time I don't even miss it.

In fact it's rather nice.
No coughs, no colds, no doctor's bills;
no running costs at all.

I can buy the Bank of England,
if I want to,
with my savings on toilet soap alone.

But the thing that bothers me is
– I daresay I'll get used to it
by the time the lease

on the library expires,
which is to say
in nine hundred and ninety-nine years –

that although I don't have a body,
much less a cock,
I sometimes get this phantom hardon

and feel as horny
as a rhino.
Very disconcerting.

3

I haven't felt the warmth
of a woman's body against mine
for a hundred years.

More. I died in the year,
let me see now, was it
five thousand six hundred and twenty-four?

– according to the Hebrew calendar, of course.
And what year is this now?
Five thousand seven hundred and forty –

six or something?
Good Lord, has it been that long
since I had a fuck?

4

I've forgotten
how to fight the fire of a woman's loins
with the fire from mine.

Forgotten how to coil my fire
around hers
in coaxial passion.

Forgotten the taste of a woman's mouth,
the feel of a belly
against mine.

Forgotten how beautifully
a man's palm
can fit a woman's crotch.

Haven't felt the tendons
on the inside of her thighs
tense under my thumb,

or sported like a dolphin
in an ocean of delight
– finned by a woman's feet.

Forgotten how,
her head pillowed on my shoulder,
arms legs and dreams entwined,

Hannah and I
used to make a perfect canoe
and just drift down the long river of night.

5

Gold and silver;
gums and spices; cotton, silks and wool;
opium, wheat and tea,

whatever moved by land or sea,
felt the hand
or bore the mark of Sassoon & Co.

My galleons sailed the Atlantic,
the Indian Ocean,
the Pacific and the China Sea.

6

Not bad, eh?
Not bad at all, I'd say,
for a Sephardic Jew,

a fugitive from Baghdad,
a runaway
who had slipped through the city gates

with nothing more than a prayer shawl,
his phylacteries,
a copy of the Pentateuch,

a money belt,
and a few pearls
sewn into the lining of his cloak;

who fled from Basra
just a jump ahead of Daud Pasha's Turks
who were after his blood;

and after some not very
spectacular adventures in Bushire,
in Persia,

where he spent the whole of his first night
shooting rats with a pistol
in a wharf-shed on the waterfront,

decided to come to these islands – where,
a fortune-teller insisted,
immense riches awaited him –

with a thousand pounds borrowed
from a family friend,
found a place to start a small counting house

in Tamarind Lane,
and threw the doors open for business
after nailing his mezuzahs to the doorpost.

7

I find myself cast in a role I detest;
that of an observer,
a spectator,

reduced to making faces,
rolling his eyes,
and sticking his tongue out occasionally

at this city that gets
more and more unrecognisable
with every passing year.

Responses
that may have to make way for tears,
for what I see now is a sick city.

A cement-eating blood-guzzling city
pissing silver, shitting gold,
and choking on its vomit.

In fact, what's happening now
is that all that shit
is beginning to come out of its mouth.

And I find myself a prisoner once again,
posthumously,
wearing a stone collar around my neck,

in Bombay instead of Baghdad,
with no hope this time
of ransom or rescue,

and forced to watch
the slow disintegration of a city
I cared about more than any other.

8

I've seen the massive rampart wall,
twenty-seven feet high and just as broad,
of the old Fort St George fall.

173

I've seen the moorish dome
of the Prince of Wales Museum grow and grow
like a monster bubble before my eyes.

I've seen the gaslights
extinguished,
along with the whole tribe of gaslighters,

and replaced by tiresome
Lady Electricity
who has robbed my nights of mystery and stars.

I've seen horsedrawn trams
come and go,
and I've seen their horseless daughters,

after a rattling reign
of sixty years or so,
follow them more noisily, into oblivion.

I've seen horseless carriages
breed like rabbits
until a plague of motor-cars chokes the streets.

9

I've seen a black horse panic,
neigh,
buckjump and leap off

a high pedestal,
a drop of nearly fifteen feet,
one manic night

in the light
of a menstruating moon,
and gallop away,

very nearly unhorsing
the poor prince in the process,
dragging him along

174

in his magnificent field-marshal's uniform,
one foot, shod
like its mate in a riding boot,

still hooked and hanging on to the stirrup,
head banging on the ground,
and the thunder of hooves

fading down Hornby Road
– or whatever they call it now –
all the way to the zoo.

But the valiant prince, from what I hear,
with true Brit grit,
managed to get back in the saddle,

and there abides
in total command of his steed
once again,

the sword still by his side,
the Order of Bath still around his neck,
the hat still in his right hand,

and head-wounds completely healed
by a poultice of bird-droppings
on his balding head.

10

Ten thousand pounds
down the drain, if you ask me.
But that's Abdulla,

that stupid son of mine,
all over again.
I refuse to call him Albert,

much less Sir Albert.
What kind of a name is that
for a descendant of David?

The equivalent of profits
from a hundred chests of opium
down the China Sea.

I could've told him even then,
on that rainy day in June
more than a hundred years ago,

when Sir Richard Temple
unveiled that
monument of sycophancy in bronze,

in the presence of some of the most
distinguished umbrellas in town,
that the statue stinks.

Which is not to take any credit
away from Boehm,
who produced a wonderful piece of work.

But there's a price to be paid
for knighthood, I guess;
and what's ten thousand pounds these days?

11

He would have made
a great Prince of Captivity,
my son Abdulla would have,

in the glory days of old Baghdad.
I can just see him –
attired in billowing robes

of embroidered silk –
enter the court
with the heralds proclaiming,

'Amilu tarik li saidna ben Daud'
– Make way
for the Prince of Captivity –

and kiss the hand of the Caliph,
just as he would,
silk-hatted and frock-coated,

kiss the hand of a queen,
the Order of the Star of India
pinned on his chest

instead of the Cypher of Mohammad
dangling
from a huge turban on his head.

12

Not far away
I keep hearing voices,
strident voices.

I strain my ears,
but I can never catch
a single word.

Just a surge and crash
of waves of anger,
an undertow of despondency.

A very fine spray
of ionised syllables
leaves a deposit of salt

in the shells of my ears
and at the roots
of my beard.

And why do I think
of an angry Tigris in spate
taking to the streets

and rushing into homes
already looted
by the Pasha's soldiers?

Man of the Year

1

Here I stand at this street corner,
leaning on the shoulder of a bright red pillar-box
at a drunken angle,

a foolish grin on my face,
an empty half-pint bottle of rum in my pocket,
a cracker up my arse,

listening to an old Elvis number
(Santa Claus is Back in Town)
coming out of a record shop.

And I feel like dancing in the street
– but I can't.
I'm incapable of such kneejerk reactions:

they've stuffed me
a little too tight for comfort, I guess,
like a forked sausage.

Head full of cottonwool,
sawdust in my gloves and socks,
a bellyful of shredded old newspapers.

2

Actually, I'm a pretty solid kind of guy.
Underneath my faded jeans,
export surplus extra large sporty jacket,

and a hat straight out of Marlboro country,
you'll find
that my head is sewn on real tight.

Take away my dashing
rainbow-coloured muffler (it's from Chor Bazar),
and you'll see what I mean.

There are thirty stitches round my neck.
Here,
you can count them if you wish.

3

It's such a lovely morning in December,
and it feels so good
just to be alive and standing here,

as if I had all the time in the world,
and watching the beautiful girls of Bombay
go by in a steady stream,

to their typewriters, switchboards, computers,
as to the impatient arms
of their waiting lovers.

But nobody knows better than I
that time
is one thing I'm running out of fast,

and my one regret is going to be this:
to leave this world
so full of girls I never kissed.

Malati, Niloufer, Anjali, Shanta,
Alpana, Kalpana, Shirin, Zarine, Sylvia, Maria,
Harlene, Yasmin, Nina, Kamala, Mona, Lopa;

I love you one and all,
and wish I could kiss a long goodbye
to each one of you, individually.

4

Inside the pillar-box,
new year greeting cards are smooching
in the permissive dark.

I hear them billing and cooing,
sighing and moaning,
as if there's no tomorrow.

They nestle against each other
in the zero gravity of pure love and affection
where all laws break down,

in the no-man's-land
between the sender and the receiver,
betraying both.

One last fling before each one goes
primly to its rightful receiver,
with clean ivory-card conscience.

5

I was a pretty unremarkable year,
all in all; and will,
no doubt, be left out of history books,

with no revolutions, wars, genocides,
no disasters, natural or otherwise,
to remember me by.

Nothing much happened, except
that the Himalayas rose by another inch,
fewer flamingoes came to Kutch,

and the leaning tower of Pisa leaned
a little further out
by another 1.29 millimetres,

the Danube poured
two hundred and three cubic kilometers
of fresh water into the Black Sea,

the hole in the ozone layer widened,
the earth became poorer
by two thousand seven hundred plant species.

I did not resolve any conflicts,
or presume to solve any
of the perennial questions of philosophy.

There were no technological breakthroughs,
no big leaps;
just a lot of hopping around on one foot.

No new ideas.
A lot of old ones served with a sizzle,
with plenty of spice to mask the rotten smell.

The good news, on the other hand,
is that schoolboys
and girls will not have to memorise me.

Who got the Nobel for literature?
Who the Booker?
Who won the cup at Wimbledon?

And who did Time magazine pick
as the Man of the Year?
I have already forgotten.

6 ENVOI

As paper trumpets blare and toot,
as sirens wail and foghorns hoot,
and as churchbells toll all around me

– I wish a happy new year to you all.

Breathing fire, coughing smoke,
spitting ash,
as firecrackers burst inside my pants

– I wish a happy new year to you all.

As all my buttons pop,
my chest opens and lungs collapse,
as a feather of flame starts eating my hat

– I wish a happy new year to you all.

As the Rajabai Tower cranes its neck
to see me reduced to a smudge on the road,
and bursts into a joyous song

– I wish a happy new year t

Traffic Lights

fifty phantom motorcyclists
all in black

crash-helmeted outriders
faceless behind tinted visors

come thundering from one end of the road
and go roaring down the other

shattering the petrified silence of the night
like a delirium of rock-drills

preceded by a wailing cherry-top
and followed by a faceless president

in a deathly white mercedes
coming from the airport and going downtown

raising a storm of protest in its wake
from angry scraps of paper and dry leaves

but unobserved by traffic lights
that seem to have eyes only for each other

and who like ill-starred lovers
fated never to meet

but condemned to live forever and ever
in each other's sight

continue to send signals to each other
throughout the night

and burn with the cold passion of rubies
separated by an empty street

Sarpa Satra

(2004)

Many thanks to my friends
Arvind Krishna Mehrotra, Adil Jussawalla
and Anand Thakore
for going over the manuscript
and making many valuable suggestions.
And many thanks indeed to Jane Bhandari
who set it up on her PC *for the love of it.*

Sarpa Satra:
According to the Mahabharata,
a sacrifice performed by Janamejaya
with the object
of annihilating the Nagas,
or the Snake People.

Janamejaya

It was a scheming snake, I'm told,
with a grudge against my great-grandfather
that killed my father.

Killed him with venom
that had gained in potency
through years of patient waiting,

that could, with a single drop,
turn a full-grown banyan tree
in a flash into a crackling cloud of ash

suspended for one endless moment
over a fluted pillar of fire
before collapsing into a smoking ruin.

A snake that had used
all the cunning of its kind to get past
the complex shield of the defences

my father, who had been warned of the conspiracy
by his secret police well ahead of time,
had surrounded himself with

– a palace perched atop a single column,
that stood like a crystal lotus
on a steel stem in the middle of a vast lake

patrolled round the clock by crocodiles
equipped with nightvision –
and which he thought was impenetrable.

Not for this assassin though,
who had had himself smuggled in,
disguised as a tiny worm in a fruitbowl

and had grown before the unbelieving eyes
of all the king's men who fled in terror
to coil himself around my father

and sting him into a searing flame
of pure pain
and turn the whole palace in fact

into one grand funeral pyre.
The killer himself, having struck,
took off like a streak

of lightning in reverse
to watch the blaze triumphantly from above
and do a little jig in the night sky.

I knew nothing of all this
at the time
– I was only a child then –

and my guardians had to wait patiently
for me to come of age
to lay this terrible piece of knowledge on me.

But now that I know,
I assure the slippery sons of Kadru
they will not get away with it.

(I hear they actually distributed sweets
in Bhogawati
when my father died.)

My vengeance will be swift and terrible.
I will not rest
until I've exterminated them all.

They'll discover
that no hole is deep enough
to hide from Janamejaya.

Jaratkaru Speaks to Her Son Aastika

1

What would your reaction be
if someone were to come up to you
and say,

My father died of snakebite.
When? Oh, I was too young then.
I don't even remember,

but I'm going to avenge his death
by killing
every single snake that lives;

yes,
by wiping out the whole species
from the face of the earth.

You'd naturally assume first
that the man was joking.
And after you realise he's not,

that he's completely serious,
you may look at him closely, perhaps,
trying to remember the name of a good shrink.

Or tell him about your own plan
to cleanse the earth of all ants
because one bit your mum.

Or try to explain to him, perhaps,
how impractical the whole idea is.
Point out the flaws in his logic.

Tell him how morally unjustifiable
his position is,
or how politically incorrect.

And, if the person voicing such sentiments
should happen to be
the king of a sizeable country,

it should be cause for concern indeed
for the future
of the country in question;

and, before such thoughts can take root
in the sovereign head
or evolve into a clear plan of action,

one might decide to do something about it.
Like leave him for a few days
at the bottom of a deep dry well

without food or water maybe
and get a host of brahmins – a thousand
may be enough –

to sit around the mouth of the well
and chant peace mantras round the clock
until he has had enough

and sues for peace.
The alternative, of course, is to depose him.
Or leave the country.

But what do the people
around Janamejaya,
his cronies and councillors, do?

Oh, they encourage him instead
(can you beat that?),
they applaud and encourage him.

And I don't mean just
Uttanka who, mind you,
has his own score to settle

with Takshaka and is only too ready
to feed this fire now
with rivers of molten butter

just as he was ready once
to blow air
up the arsehole of a firehorse.

But I mean all the great
sages as well.
Yes, they actually encourage him

and invent a yajnya
– a complete innovation –
called the Snake Sacrifice

just for his convenience.
What will they think of next?
One wonders.

Vedic sanction for the thread ceremony
of a hyena's son?
Done.

And, once that is settled,
the sort of thing that quickly balloons
into a question of national importance

would seem to be:
who will bag the contract for constructing
the sacrificial township?

And no one has the time,
but no one,
to listen to what Lohitaksha has to say

(that Saturn in the asterism
of Uttaraphalguni
does not bode well for the project),

once the king himself has dismissed
the architect's warning
as so much superstitious nonsense.

All the great rishis and maharishis,
so-called
great thinkers, all

the finest minds of our age,
even people like
Atreya, Uddalaka, Shvetaketu

– people we thought of
until, oh, the day before yesterday
as living volcanoes of conscience

ready to blow their tops
at the first sign
of any wrongdoing in the land

or whenever the mighty strayed
from the path of justice –
seem strangely silent

and worried about just one thing:
how to wangle a job for themselves
as officiating priests.

Sad, isn't it,
that even someone like Somashravas
is unable to hide

how very pleased with himself he is
because he has managed
to land the plum job

of presiding priest
(and at such a young age too!);
but why deny him the right?

He deserves the job. And, besides,
it's not every day that the king himself
comes to you with a blank cheque

and all but begs you
on bended knees to accept the offer.
How can anyone refuse?

Somashravas, you say?
But his own mother is a snake woman,
isn't she? Sure!

And so?
Should he allow a little thing like that
to stand between himself

and the highest pinnacle of success
that any mantra mutterer
can hope to aspire to?

And the heart sinks
when you realise that even someone
like the great Vyasa himself

looks upon the event,
essentially,
as a not-to-be-missed opportunity

to unleash his self-indulgent epic
on an unsuspecting world
– way too long if you ask me.

I mean 24000 verses, Lord have mercy!
what it badly needs
is a good editor.

But, then again,
where else can he hope to get
such an audience, handpicked,

consisting of the best minds
of three generations
– crème de la crème, oh, absolutely –

and a captive one at that
for so long a period of time?
Not again in this avatara, for sure!

But what did you expect of
an old man
who saw it as no part of his business

to interfere, let alone try
and stop
the madness of his grandchildren

from getting completely out of hand;
who let it run
its full course to the inevitable

tragic ending;
saw them all kill each other off;
just stood by

as a whole nation destroyed itself
and, instead of being
ashamed

of the whole saga
and his own role in it,
or trying to forget it all,

quietly set out
to put down the whole wretched chronicle
in black and white

and in polished verse
to the eternal shame of
posterity.

2

Which is not to say that I
have ever been able to forgive Takshaka
for what he did.

To say that he was always an extremist
is not to make excuses for him.
He deserves the harshest punishment in the book.

And I certainly do not approve
of the way he's hiding now
behind Indra's throne to save his skin,

hoping his powerful friend
will help him escape the consequences
of an act we're now paying for.

It only shows what cowards
all terrorists are
behind their snarling ferocious masks.

But, to tell you the truth,
Takshaka has never been quite himself
since his wife died.

Cut down brutally
during the senseless massacre that took place
when...

But you don't know about that, do you?
You don't know anything
about how they torched the Khandava forest.

You wouldn't.
In fact we've all been trying to forget it,
erase the incident from our memories.

But I think it's time you learnt.
You should know
what really happened – it's your right –

before venerable Vyasa gives
his own spin
to the whole of human history.

You must have heard
of Janamejaya's great-grandfather –
Arjuna, the great superhero.

A wizard with a bow,
he had no equal in archery,
unless it was Kama.

But he received divine weapons
– a divine bow,
two inexhaustible quivers –

and god knows what happened to him,
what came over him!
Just went berserk, I guess.

For the very first act of heroism
he performed
as soon as he got the new toys in his hands

was, well, this:
he burnt down one of the largest
rainforests in the land,

and what a thorough job he made of it.
Reduced it completely
to ash.

It wasn't just him,
no.
He was aided in this crime

by another.
A crosscousin of his,
a crony since childhood.

They were a team of sorts,
partners
in many escapades.

This other
had also acquired
divine weapons of his own:

a chakra called
Sudarshan
and a gada called Kaumodaki.

And it was these two together
that did this thing
– burn down the Khandava forest.

And when they were done,
not one green leaf,
not a single blade of grass

was left behind.
Just miles of ash that kept smouldering
for months afterwards.

Surging with sap
and bursting with gums and resins,
that forest had been

God's own laboratory on earth
where life had been allowed to express itself
with complete abandon.

It contained five thousand
different kinds of butterflies alone
and a golden squirrel found nowhere else.

Some of the trees in that place
were, oh,
hundreds and hundreds of years old, easily;

and it contained a wealth
of medicinal plants
that were not found anywhere else.

But nothing was left, not a trace
of that great sanctuary so dear to Indra
and protected by the gods themselves.

By the time these two were done,
it was all gone,
everything.

Not just the trees, birds, insects and animals
(herds upon herds
of elephants, gazelles, antelopes),

but people, Aastika,
people as well.
Simple folk,

children of the forest
who had lived there happily for generations,
since time began.

They've gone without a trace.
With their language
that sounded like the burbling of a brook,

their songs that sounded like the twitterings of birds,
and the secrets of their shamans
who could cure any sickness

by casting spells with their special flutes
made from the hollow
wingbones of red-crested cranes.

Why did they do it?
Who knows!
Just for kicks, maybe.

Maybe just the fact
that now they had all these fantastic weapons
went to their heads

and they just couldn't wait
to test their awesome powers.
Maybe they just wanted

a clear title to the land,
unchallenged
by so much as a tigermoth.

They were certainly determined to make sure
that nothing got out
of that conflagration alive.

The moment anything tried,
they drove it back into that inferno
or mowed it down,

as the two of them
thundered around the burning forest
in their divine chariots.

Trumpeting elephants
rushing towards water
for safety

trample on half-cooked turtles
as they crawl out of
the boiling lakes.

A gazelle trips over
a dead crab at the water's edge
and sprains an ankle.

The taste of honey
still on its tongue,
a bear bursts into flames,

falls from a tree
with a burning branch between its legs
to roll in the flaming grass below.

The chakra slices
every single honeybee
from a swarm in flight

and returns to the tip
of Krishna's finger
for fresh instructions.

A hundred arrows leave
Partha's bow
all at the same time

to go after a flock
of a hundred swans
winging its way to safety

and (well done!)
do not miss
even one.

Look, Arjuna!
See that lioness
with her mane in flames?

Don't let her get away
just because
she has a cub in her mouth.

Oh, good!
You got them both
with a single shaft.

And where, you may well ask,
was Takshaka
when all this was happening?

In Kurukshetra, if you please!
And what was he doing there?
Having a dip

in the holy Saraswati river
to fulfil a vow,
as he claims?

Or spending a night
in the arms of a Puluvan girl
he was involved with at the time,

as I suspect? Never mind.
What is certain is that
he was not where he was needed most:

to defend his wife and son,
and protect
the forest he held in trust for the gods.

For although his son got away
– a miraculous escape –
his wife was not so lucky

and fell prey to a shaft
that came from the magical quiver
of the valiant Arjuna.

When he came to see me
that time, after killing Parikshita,
to brag about

how infernally clever he had been
and what a mighty blow he had struck
in the name of justice,

hoping to wow an impressionable
kid-sister and to bask
in her wide-eyed admiration,

I had to disappoint him.
I was only
horrified at what he had done.

What I don't understand,
I said to him, is
where have you been all this time?

Why did you not make Arjuna
pay for his crime
while he was yet alive?

And God knows he lived long enough –
in fact so feeble had he become
in his old age, I am told,

that he couldn't even hold
a bow in his hands.
You could easily have seized your chance then.

Why did you wait
for his grandson to grow up
to give him a taste of your terrible poison

instead of Arjuna.
Don't you know
that true revenge accepts no substitute?

3

Marutta, I know,
had tried it before
– the wholesale destruction of snakes –

but not like this.
He never dignified his slaughter
with the high-sounding name

of sacrifice
nor carried it out with the full blessings
of vedic event managers,

complete with song and dance,
fun and games,
gambling and chariot races,

and Vaishampayana reciting
the Mahabharata
with his own embellishments

as snake after snake
goes to his doom in the sacrificial fire
and is burnt alive.

A nice yajnya, this.
Not a single sacrificial post in sight.
No ropes, no knives.

There's no need for the queen,
or anybody else,
to lead the animal to the killing field

and take its life by smothering it
bludgeoning it,
or worse.

No need to carve up the parts
– omentum, liver, lung, bladder,
genitals –

and cook them separately;
or to roast
the victim's still-bleeding heart on a spit.

Oh no. Nothing of the sort.
Nothing crude.
It's all sorcery: mantras do it all.

Snakes from near and far,
large and small,
come floating, writhing through the air,

dragged by spells,
as if caught in an invisible lasso,
and throw themselves into the fire.

The more you feed it
the hungrier it seems to get
and the higher it blazes,

Oh for God's sake!
Is this a yajnya
or some kind of a snakecharmers' convention!

Surely this sacrifice
is not pleasing
in the sight of the gods!

How could it be
when they haven't even been
invited for it.

No, it wasn't an oversight,
They would do well
to stay away from it.

For they could easily end up
as the victims
in this cynical yajnya

if they came anywhere
near it.
And they know it.

Can you think of a worse insult
to Agni,
the sacred sacrificial fire,

whose pleasant duty it is to carry
gifts, oblations,
supplications and praise

offered lovingly by man
to God (or the gods concerned) and
bring back their blessings,

than to give him the dirty job
of a common
assassin, butcher or a mass murderer,

to employ him
to exterminate an entire species
systematically

and in cold blood
in violation of all the known laws
of gods and man,

to offer hecatombs to
– what! –
one man's twisted logic and madness?

This snake sacrifice,
this mockery, this grotesque parody
of the institution of yajnya

has got to stop.
But all those who should have realised this
are on the payroll of Janamejaya

and will do nothing to spoil his party.
The very people
who one would've thought

had enough sense of decency
to hang their heads in shame
at what's going on

turn out to be
the chief actors in this theatre
of the macabre

and are all busy playing
the various roles allotted to them
not only without

the slightest trace of embarrassment
but with evident relish
as they go about their tasks importantly,

mumbling mantras or whatever,
and looking oh so dapper in black
– black dhotis, black shawls

and black pigskin slippers to match,
in which their vedic
costume designers have dressed them

with such uncanny appropriateness –
as rivers of snakefat
sputter, sizzle and flow ceaselessly

and the sickening smell of burning snakeflesh
– strong enough to make you gag –
continues to spread throughout the land.

It has, by now, become so
pervasive,
so much a part of the air we breathe

that soon we'll start thinking of fresh air
as something unindian, alien
and antinational.

Have they all gone mad?
What do they think they're doing,
these wise men!

Does one have to remind them
that this
planet itself, this sphere, our whole earth

is resting,
balanced precariously,
on the hood of a snake called Shesha,

the mightiest of them all?
(And yes,
I'm proud to say it – he's my brother.

Every year I send him a rakhi
to remind him of his little sister:
me!)

Don't they realise what will happen
if, God forbid, he gets wind,
even the tiniest whiff,

of what's going on?
For he's not going to like it one bit,
I can tell you that.

And that, surely, will be The End.
Of not just the nagas, or any one species,
but of everything and everybody.

A slight toss of his head...
the merest shrug...
and it will be all over.

Khatam.
That's what I'm really worried about.
And once that happens,

THEN what!
Surely the time has come
for someone to go

and ask Janamejaya,
that bull among men,
one simple question:

once the earth goes bust,
what speck of dust
do you intend to rule on, Mr King?

And I think it's *your* job,
Aastika.
I mean who else is there to do it?

It becomes your responsibility
automatically
just because nobody else wants it,

not even the gods.
And something tells me
that you're exactly the right man for it.

You're too young
– true.
Still wet behind the ears,

some may say.
But that
actually may be your greatest strength.

It means your eyesight
is good,
your vision clear.

Not spoilt by reading too many books yet,
or ruined
by the smoke of too many sacrifices,

or clouded by rage, power, ego, pride
or any of the other
common diseases of the eye.

It means your brain is not maggoty yet,
with perceived wrongs,
or pickled in the brine of hatred.

It means your wounds heal quickly,
thank God for that.
It means you do not view the world

through the dark prism of a wound
infected
by the dirty bandage of history.

It means that the gangrene
of insensitivity
hasn't spread to your soul.

But then, of course, you don't have to go
just because
your mother feels you should.

If you think it's a stupid idea,
just say so
and I'll shut up.

If you think so,
it really must be so.
I've total faith in your judgement.

All these things that are happening
have no doubt affected
my ability to think straight.

Go there and do
– what?
I should have asked myself

that simple question.
I must be out of my mind
to suggest it.

You'll be completely lost
in all the confusion
– if you're able to get in, that is.

Which itself is doubtful
They'll stop you at the gate and turn you away.
Or worse:

insult you.
Janamejaya's goons will beat you up
and throw you out.

We all know what happened to Sarama's son,
how they beat him up
for no fault of his.

But then,
what other alternative
do we have?

Just sit back
and watch this holocaust
until the last snake on earth

goes to his doom?
The way we did last night
as we all sat on the terrace talking

(about – what else? –
is there any other subject anyone
ever talks about these days?),

when Kakshak and Pishang,
your cousins,
playmates you grew up with,

were snatched away
suddenly from our midst,
right before our eyes,

as if an invisible eagle
had swooped down
and picked them up in his talons.

And we just sat there gaping helplessly
and watched
the two of them until

– trying to hang on to each other
desperately
and looking like a squirming Om sign –

they disappeared
in the direction of Taxila
(the sky above the city

that lies just beyond the horizon
is always red these days,
like the eyes of a priest

from continuous exposure
to holy smoke
and excessive drinking of soma),

to plunge into the same fire
of revenge
that had swallowed Hiranyavaha,

Pradyot, Chakra, Purna, Prahas, Paila,
Mandalaka, Kaladanta,
and countless others before them;

and in which, sooner or later,
Vasuki
and I myself will end up as burnt offerings.

Look up, Aastika.
Look up, my son.
Over there...

There goes another naga family
(clinging to each other,
they look like a swan, a suicidal swan)

in search of the source
of this unholy river of dirty smoke
that has poisoned the whole

atmosphere in this land.
Was that Manas you think?
I think it was.

Manas and his wife.
Pingalakshi – was that her name? –
and their two little children.

They seemed determined
to stay together till the very end.
Not to be separated.

But their grip on each other
appeared to slacken by degrees -
did you also feel that?

Who next?
Well, it's anybody's guess,
but I hope it's me

and not Vasuki.
Of all my brothers it's he
who has always meant the most to me;

and I just couldn't bear
to see him suffer.
Not great Vasuki, the great serpent king

who coiled himself around
Mount Mandara once
to churn up the ocean for gods and demons.

You were his favourite nephew, his pet.
I think he loved you more
than his own children – Kakshak and Chakra.

Remember how he used to carry you
piggyback
and take you for a ride around the world

mostly to Mount Gandhamadana,
that playground of the gods
that both of you loved so much?

I hope it's my turn next.
Hope I'm snatched away before him.
But... no such luck.

It's going to be him, I'm afraid.
He hasn't said a word
for three days – it's unlike him.

And look, how restless he is.
I think the heat
is slowly getting to him.

At least there's one good thing,
I tell myself
– and find consolation in the thought

that you have nothing to fear,
nothing to fear.
You'll be safe, absolutely.

For although I have given you birth,
although a snake woman
has brought you into this world,

you are your father's son.
A man.
You belong to the human race.

Don't forget that, ever.
And that's the reason
why you'll have to stop this sacrifice.

Not for Vasuki Mama's sake,
or mine.
Not for anything else –

but to make sure
that the last vestige of humanity
you are heir to,

your patrimony, yes,
does not go up in smoke
in this yajnya.

Go, Aastika;
and my prayers go with you.
Go, my son,

and all our hopes
go with you.
My heart tells me

you'll find a way
to put a stop
to that festival of hatred.

The Ritual Bath

When these sacrificial jamborees
come to an end,
the officiating priests,

honoured guests, vedic wizards
and other
intellectual superstars of the show

go back to their respective homes,
ashramas or whatever,
bearing wealth beyond measure –

cartloads of gold,
herds of cattle with golden horns,
slavegirls dripping pearls.

Bands of brahmins,
hangers-on,
and assorted freeloaders

strip the place
of everything that isn't nailed down
and make off

with whatever they can lay
their hands on –
sacrificial vessels, furniture, deerskins, bricks.

After the mandatory
ritual bath
to mark the conclusion of the sacrifice,

kings return to their capitals,
reminding themselves
that they also have kingdoms to govern,

wondering
which neighbourly kingdoms to attack next
or what new taxes to levy

to refill the coffers,
and ask their ministers to come up
with recommendations.

When these things come to an end,
people find
other subjects to talk about

than just
the latest episode of the Mahabharata
and the daily statistics of death;

rediscover simpler pleasures –
fly kites,
collect wild flowers, make love.

Life seems
to return to normal.
But do not be deceived.

Though, sooner or later,
these celebrations of hatred too
come to an end

like everything else,
the fire – the fire lit for the purpose –
can never be put out.

The fire that Aurva got up,
for example,
to avenge the massacre of the Bhrugus,

still burns at the bottom of the sea,
where he threw it
at the instance of his ancestors.

And the fire that Parashara produced
for the destruction
of rakshasas

still rages, they say,
in the great forest beyond
the Himalayas

where the great sage tried
to dispose of it
when he stopped the sacrifice

at the urgings of Poulastya;
and there, to this day,
they say, it continues to consume

rakshasas
rocks
trees

The Boatride and other poems

(2009)

NOTE ON THE TEXT

For previously published poems and translations, the text is taken from the magazine or anthology where the work first appeared. Obvious errors, however, have been corrected and details of first publication are given in the Notes. For some of the unpublished material, particularly the translations from *Chirimiri* and of Tukaram, which I came across in Kolatkar's papers after his death, I took Adil Jussawalla's help before finalising the text. Sometimes there were two or three drafts of the same poem, but, more often, the alternatives were given in the margin. This could be a word, a phrase, or an entire line. It was Kolatkar's practice never to scratch anything out, so the alternatives did not necessarily indicate a preference. Adil and I had, in May 2004, edited *Kala Ghoda Poems* and *Sarpa Satra*, and we followed the same editorial principle we had adopted then. The principle was a simple one: to rely on our judgment. Except that then there was Kolatkar to double-check with, in case we had erred. And in one case we had. Needless to say, all editorial responsibility, finally, is mine alone.

AKM

I Poems in English 1953-1967

The Renunciation of the Dog

Tell me why the night before we started
        Dogs were vainly
                Barking at the waves;
And tell my why in an unknown temple
        Days and waves away
                A black dog dumbly
From out of nowhere of ourselves yawned and leapt;
        And leaving us naked
                And shamefaced,
Tell me why the black dog died
        Intriguingly between
                God and our heads.

Of an origin moot as cancer's

Of an origin moot as cancer's,
A terribly nominal horse. He trod
Like a rumour of a raid.
Though his hoof-told tale rang frank as bread

The narrative dexterity of his rhyming hooves
Of the Clever Hans variety
Alarmed, as a spate of counterfeit currency
Does. And startled

For the first time out of their customary torpor,
Mountains – the outdated immortals, the ageing
Stone age majesties – moved, to migrate.

And the clop clop coins on the way, by him
Lavished, were left untouched
And innocent looking like an explosive cigarette.

Dual

A man and a woman in a radical cage
Grope and get bruised in an animal light.
They get their crumbs from amused spectators:
The spectacled leopard, the highbrow camel
And the high heeled deer.

The unlearnt skin of the two, so dazzled
in the narcotic light, is blunt and smooth
like the fat palm of an infant cactus.
The two might declare harsh thorns and live
as insensate as a cactus, piteously bristled
and opposing the light.

In a godforsaken hotel

In a godforsaken hotel
in a godforsaken town
lizards will cast
my horoscope
on the walls of a room
that's next door to death's.

In a godforsaken hotel
in a godforsaken town
a spider will watch
me masturbate
from the sneering corner
of a neurotic.

In a godforsaken hotel
in a godforsaken town
I keep myself waiting
behind a door
that will open when my shoe
creaks in the corridor.

In a godforsaken hotel
in a godforsaken town
I mean to set
fire to my ape
between the four walls
of a starved and lonely room.

Make Way Poet

make way poet, jaywalking,
for evolution's automobile
or in its homicidal headlights
wither with a smile.

hey beggar, proud as a loaf
of bread, you there;
bright stations of star-lice
based in your hair

of dishevelled death, your breath
smelling of words, you'll sprawl
on a timeside pavement
– a dumbstruck hairy stall.

The Hag

Death pins his abstraction like a rare but ugly
butterfly on her brain. Tells an off colour
joke. She laughs, of necessity, a little vaguely.

The hag is stone deaf: you wouldn't even guess.
The window has a curtain. It's florid. It's grimy.
Entrenched behind it she devours oranges

In self defence. She likes them baggy. She paws.
She claws. An orange isn't peeled. It's torn. Each
fruit a vapid debacle. An invalid pose

in tattered filigree. The hag incites her mandibles
to mob and maul a piece. Her entire face
converges in a featureless fury rushes to the battle's

toothless centre. Eyes. Like a dead horse
on a battlefield her eyes deny the avid farce.

Woman

a woman may collect cats read thrillers
her insomnia may seep through the great walls of history
a lizard may paralyse her
a sewing machine may bend her
moonlight may intercept the bangle
circling her wrist

a woman may name her cats
the circulating library
may lend her new thrillers

a spiked man may impale her
a woman may add
a new recipe to her scrapbook

judiciously distilling her whimper the city lights
may declare it null and void
in a prodigious weather
above a darkling woman
surgeons may shoot up and explode
in a weather fraught with forceps
a woman may damn
man

a woman may shave her legs regularly
a woman may take up landscape painting
a woman may poison
23 cockroaches

Suicide of Rama

winding verses stir him up
the turreted epic shrugs him off
the river resumes him
from legend's ledge the hero falls

the crescent cuts a rope of fables
we cloud the skeleton with folklore
from valmiki's rooftop rama jumps
disturbing a tile or two

his flesh of myth saponified
his arse turned up toward the moon
rama drifts like a gourd
far from sap or shore

man leaves his legend standing
one wave bears the other out
the river refers his bones
to the salt judgement of the sea

Irani Restaurant Bombay

the cockeyed shah of iran watches the cake
decompose carefully in a cracked showcase;
distracted only by a fly on the make
as it finds in a loafer's wrist an operational base.

dogmatically green and elaborate trees defeat
breeze; the crooked swan begs pardon
if it disturb the pond; the road, neat
as a needle, points at a lovely cottage with a garden.

the thirsty loafer sees the stylised perfection
of the landscape, in a glass of water, wobble.
a sticky tea print for his scholarly attention
singles out a verse from the blank testament of the table.

an instant of mirrors turns the tables on space.
while promoting darkness below the chair, the cat
in its two timing sleep dreams evenly and knows
dreaming to be an administrative problem. his cigarette

lit, the loafer, affecting the exactitude of a pedagogue,
places the burnt matchstick in the tea circle; and sees it rise:
as when to identify a corpse one visits a morgue
and politely the corpse rises from a block of ice.

the burnt matchstick with the tea circle makes a rude
compass. the heretic needle jabs a black star.
tables chairs mirrors are night that needs to be sewed
and cashier is where at seams it comes apart.

Visit to a Doctor

Finally you get there
by land by sea by air
and with nothing to show
for thirty years of go
and get, of love and hate,
but an X-ray plate.

You have an appointment
you explain to the attendant,
a decrepit old goat
who repeats your name
as if it were a lame
excuse to clear his throat.

You send in your card
and sit on your guard
between a potted plant
and someone else's aunt.
You think the room is normal;
in fact it's hexagonal.

You are led before the doc
and, seated, begin to talk:
your weight is going down,
your appetite is bad.
He listens with a frown,
reminding you of dad.

today I feel I do not belong

today i feel i do not belong
don't you feel like that sometimes?
   then come along man come along
   unzip the briefcase bring out the booze
   and pour me a drink as i polish my gong
   i mean to beat it black and blue
   till it's a limp and sad oblong

      bonggggg

i'm god's gift to advertising
is the refrain of my song

how is your migraine these days paul?
and what the hell is eosinophilia?
   my ulcers are bad and that is not all
   don't breathe a word to anyone about it
   but something is wrong with my right ball
   my tongue is coated my breath is bad
   it's no use gargling with dettol

      bonggggg

i'm god's gift to advertising
is the refrain of my song

you really think i'm a success
o i don't know what to think
   i'm no more sure what my sex is
   i feel i'm going round in circles
   but no – the thought presumes an axis
   what am i like? open and see
   precisely nothing in a lot of boxes

      bonggggg

i'm god's gift to advertising
is the refrain of my song

Teeth

Lord I am revealed
How my teeth gleam
My sides ache. My forehead
Yawns. I have unlocked
Like a monstrous
Pomegranate. Do not
Touch me God do not
Come near me, for all
Is grist to my grinding.

My loin has bared its teeth.
My thighs open like iron
Maidens. Guts whip out.
My nose crawls over me
Like a prehistoric
Lizard come back to life.
My throat nibbles at my
Tonsils. And I grin
Having chewed off my lips.

Dreaming of Snakes

how i forget but i escaped
that is what matters
it was an iron snake ripping
my long trail to tatters
if we run into each other
i know he will laugh
where were we he will say and
start where we left off
at any hour i will know him
in any city or town
without ever mistaking his
smile for a frown
what is my subconscious up to
and what the devil
does it mean must it always
speak in parables

i dream of pencils that wiggle
out of my fist
not to crawl down the desk but
to climb up my wrist
reptiles all sorts of them
self winding cobras
and boa constrictors disguised
as candelabras
automatic skipping ropes and
somersaulting vipers
rattlesnakes on motorcycles
chasing me their piper
they will burst out of the bedroom
the pythons the adders
and in the toilet or in a taxi
there will be no ladders

my son is dead

my son is dead
the letter began
unusual boy
in many ways
for his age yes
it mentioned how
in seven months
the baby grew as many teeth
i now believe
in heaven
it said
my son cannot
be just nowhere
the envelope
contained also
a photograph
my son is dead

My name is Arun Kolatkar

My name is Arun Kolatkar
I had a little matchbox

I lost it
then I found it
I kept it
in my right hand pocket

It is still there

Directions

Postbox

go straight
turn left
turn right
turn left
turn left
    and there is the postbox

Photographer

move your head
slightly to the left
not so much
look into the camera
smile

2, Brabourne Road

where is 2, brabourne road

Discipline

left
right
left
right
left turn
right turn
about turn
left
right
halt
attention
stand at ease
dismiss

II Poems in Marathi

One seldom sees a woman

one seldom sees a woman
more misshapen than you
but i think i owe you a poem
let's suppose the debt paid with this poem

coming right down to it
what will i write about you
at the most i could say
you loved dumb animals
and leave it that
because i saw you only once
you were feeding carrots
to a horse
and the way you stood
was as much without grace and glamour
as an empty frig in a junk shop
for a moment the saliva of the horse
glittered on your finger like a wedding ring
then the wind dropped

The Fuse

A rotten smell was coming from somewhere.
I gagged and reached for the handkerchief in my pocket
when my little finger dropped to the floor.
I picked it up with one hand
pressed the handkerchief to my nose with the other
when my nose came off. I wrapped it up
in the folds of the handkerchief and stuffed it in my pocket.

That rotten smell was still very much in the air.
The nose twitched in my pocket.
I thought I'll take a closer look and see
if there were any maggots in my little finger.
That's when the fuse went.

Three Cups of Tea

1

i wan't my pay i said
     to the manager
you'll get paid said
     the manager
but not before the first
       don't you know the rules?
   coolly i picked up his
     wristwatch
   that lay on the table
     wanna bring in the cops
       i said
'cordin to my rules
   listen baby
     i get paid when i say so

2

   allow me beautiful
i said to my sister in law
   to step in my brother's booties
     you had it coming said rehman
   a gun in his hand
    shoot me punk
kill your brother i said
    for a bloody cunt

3

i went to burma
            where the film aag was running
                        i went to see the film
the guy behind the
            booking office window
                        wants to see my passport
                                    i said
                        all i wanna do
                        is see a fucking film man
i was arrested and sent back
                        to manipur
no passport
                        the police commissioner asked
why did you go to burma?
                        prickface i said
            what's there in india?

Song of the Flour Mill

rollers spin inside my body
driven by belts of breath
watch it fellows
mind your turbans

whoever you are, woman,
brahmin, ghatan, whatever,
makes no difference
tuck your sari and scram

flee, go home to your momma
i don't even want to know
whether you're a young woman
or an old bag

whether you're dagdu, thondu or pandu
a man, a woman or a eunuch
black, white, fat or thin
is all one to me my friend

but do yourself a favour
drop your jowar
and run
run for your life

back off boss
and keep your distance
unless you want to end up
in a sack of flour

it's gone kill-crazy now, this mill
and it's not going to be satisfied
until it has ripped
every hand that feeds it

chugchug chugchug chugchug
the mill swallowed the mother of us all
swallowed her whole
in just one gulp

and what did she taste like
sweet? bitter? sour?
the mill doesn't know
and the mill doesn't care

The Turnaround

Bombay made me a beggar.
Kalyan gave me a lump of jaggery to suck.
In a small village that had a waterfall
but no name
my blanket found a buyer
and I feasted on just plain ordinary water.

I arrived in Nasik with
peepul leaves between my teeth.
There I sold my Tukaram
to buy myself some bread and mince.
When I turned off Agra Road,
one of my sandals gave up the ghost.

I gave myself a good bath
in a little stream.
I knocked on the first door I came upon,
asked for a handout, and left the village.
I sat down under a tree,
hungry no more but thirsty like never before.

I gave my name et cetera
to a man in a bullock cart
who hated beggars and quoted Tukaram,
but who, when we got to his farm later,
was kind enough to give me
a cool drink of water.

Then came Rotegaon
where I went on trial
and had to drag the carcass away
when howling all night
a dog died in the temple
where I was trying to get some sleep.

There I got bread to eat all right
but a woman was pissing.
I didn't see her in the dark
and she just blew up.
Bread you want you motherfucker you blind cunt, she said,

237

I'll give you bread.
I could smell molasses boiling in a field.
I asked for some sugarcane to eat.
I shat on vishnukranta
and wiped my arse with neem leaves.
I found a beedi lying on the road
and put it in my pocket.

It was walk walk walk and walk all the way.
It was a year of famine.
I saw a dead bullock.
I crossed a hill.
I picked up a small coin
from a temple on top of that hill.

Kopargaon is a big town.
That's where I read that Stalin was dead.
Kopargaon is a big town
where it seemed shameful to beg.
And I had to knock on five doors
to get half a handful of rice.

Dust in my beard, dust in my hair.
The sun like a hammer on the head.
An itching arse.
A night spent on flagstones.
My tinshod hegira
was hotting up.

The station two miles ahead of me,
the town three miles behind,
I stopped to straighten my dhoti
that had bunched up in my crotch
when sweat stung my eyes
and I could see.

A low fence by the roadside.
A clean swept yard.
A hut. An old man.
A young woman in a doorway.
I asked for some water
and cupped my hands to receive it.

Water dripping down my elbows
I looked at the old man.
The goodly beard.
The contentment that showed in his eyes.
The cut up can of kerosene
that lay prostrate before him.

Bread arrived, unbidden,
with an onion for a companion.
I ate it up.
I picked up the haversack I was sitting on.
I thought about it for a mile or two.
But I knew already

that it was time to turn around.

Biograph

Knotting the cord, the midwife said,
It's a boy, it's a boy, it's a boy.
Piercing an earlobe, the goldsmith said,
Two bucks, just two bucks.
Syringe in hand, the nurse said,
It's not gonna hurt, not a bit.

Measuring my dick, Baban said,
Mine's bigger, bigger than yours.
Punching my back, Baban said,
My dad can lick your dad.
Kicking my shin, Baban said,
Sissy, a sissy, what a sissy you are.

Pressing her toes against mine, Bunny said,
Bicycle, bicycle, let's play bicycle.
Rubbing spittle on my tummy, Bunny said,
Doctor, doctor, let's play doctor.
Tickling my ribs, Bunny said,
Come on in, between the sheets.

Boxing my ears, a teacher said,
How much is thirty three times thirty eight?
Rapping my knuckles, a teacher said,
And where's Sheffield then? Where's Sheffield?
Squeezing my thigh, a teacher said,
Let's go to the mango grove.

Twisting my neck, the barber said,
Don't move now, don't move.
Measuring my chest, the tailor said,
Thirty one inches, just thirty one.
Forcing my foot into the shoe, the cobbler said,
Use it, and it won't be so tight.

Jumping on my back, junior said,
Giddyup, giddyup.
Giving me the boot, my boss said,
I can't help it Mr Nene, I just can't.
Grabbing my cock, my wife said,
I'll chop it off one day, just chop it off.

Feeling my balls, a doctor said,
Hydrocele, I'm sure it's hydrocele.
Sticking a pin in my toe, another said,
Leprosy, you can take it from me, it's leprosy.
Tapping my stomach, a third one said,
Ulcer, ulcer, no doubt about it.

Stepping on my toes, a guy said,
Sorry man, I'm sorry.
Sticking an umbrella in my eye, another said,
I hope you aren't hurt.
Bearing down on me full tilt, a trucker said,
Can't you see where you going you motherfucker?

The Wind Song

Fuck your cap.
If it's gone, it's gone.
You've still got your head on, right?
Hold on to it tight.
And look after yourself, man.
A dangerwind is blowing.
Look at all this rubbish in my hair
and damn this dust,
it's all getting in my eyes!

A window shuts with a bang
And showers glass on a fat mattress.
Chandeliers have too many problems of their own
to notice how the carpets have begun
to roll up by themselves.
A Ming vase, overturned,
spins around and rolls from side to side
on a newly waxed floor
as it wrestles with a private demon if its own.

A nylon sari slithers off the clothesline
and goes swirling up in the air,
pursued by the pyjamas
of a Bengali chartered accountant,
that tear themselves away from the balcony railing
and, pedalling furiously, ascend to heaven
to catch up with the sari
and conduct a series of joint manoeuvres
high above the city skyline.

Like illiterate teleprinters
invented by a race of giants
before they could discover electricity,
rooftops come to life;
and the news of the coming storm is relayed from roof to roof
as tiles start talking in tongues.
Let me help you sweep the floor, Mr Kulkarni;
your college degrees,
they're all lying shattered on the ground.

Larry, Larry my boy,
has your dad been missing from his silver picture frame?
I thought I saw him running around in circles
around a fire hydrant in Apollo Street.
Last I saw him he was about to get into a fight
over a cute little piece of tinfoil
with three almond leaves,
two bus tickets and yards of carbon paper
that had ganged up on him.

Your poem, professor;
you say it's gone?
Slipped out of your hands and disappeared?
Just like that?
May be it went for a walk, you know.
Have you looked everywhere?
And don't look so sad, professor, cheer up!
May be the poem was never any good to begin with.
Have you considered that?

Drop the paint brush.
Leave your cans of paint and run, painter, run!
I hope you're fast on your feet.
The long legged foxy lady you painted on the billboard
has begun to shake her hips;
and I hope you're far away when she starts looking for you,
slicing her way through everything
that lies in her flight path
like a guillotine unhinged.

Teacher, teacher, look, the map!
The map of India!
The way it's kicking,
the way it's dancing on the classroom wall.
Do you think it's going to fall?
There it goes, it's gone already.
Cities, mountains, forests, rivers and all,
gone,
out the window and up into the sky.

Hospital Poems

1 *Temperature normal. Pulse, respiration satisfactory*

i lean back in the armchair
and bombay sinks

the level of the balcony parapet rises
and the city is submerged

the terraces the chimneys the watertanks the antennas
everything

the whole city
gone under

i look at what remains
my eyes take up the slack of the twilit sky

i count a crow and three sparrows
each flying according to its light

i stretch my legs
i put my feet up on the parapet

i hear a cheeping sound
i see a sparrow

is there a connection
i am afraid i do not know

this cross i make of my own two feet
floats on the last horizon

2 *Gastrojejunostomy* + *Vagotomy* + *Appendicectomy* + *Hydrocele*

how clean am i become
now you can lay me down on that pushcart
and cover me up with a clean white sheet

from neck to knee have i
been shaven clean
a stomach pump has washed my stomach out
fifteen times
enemata have purified my intestines

i feel sinless
like a grain of white rice
cooked in the holy water of the ganga

please
will you be good enough to pass me that handkerchief
thank you
there was a bit of dirt in my nose

yes
now you can lay me out on that pushcart
and cover me up with that clean white sheet

3 *Glucose/saline 500 cc*

leaving sister carol in the arms
of surgeon griffith on page thirty-two
sister sethna comes to my bedside
and takes an ounce of water in the syringe

the ryles tube comes out of my nose and puts
a question mark around my mother
reading ramdas at the other end of the room
i give the fat book in her lap a brotherly look

an ice cold exclamation mark sticks in my throat
the fifth bottle of saline is empty
sister sethna hangs the sixth one on the stand
the last one   i love you carol   and i love you too

says carol one two three four five
the drop of saline that follows the drop of saline
in the little tube of glass has become
the centre of my universe   o my right arm

my mother leaves her ramdas on the table
she comes over and stands beside my bed
the thirteenth drop of saline shines
like a perfect teardrop against her cheek

press your legs? she asks   no i tell her
i cannot see her left eye through her glasses
i see instead an open window   an overcast sky
and what i take to be a bird in flight

ramdas complains   pages kick in the air
life is a sapling of sorrow   life is an ocean of grief
life is a mountain of fear that will not move
my mother goes back and takes ramdas in her arms

these drops of saline have made a clock out of me
a clock that never runs down and where time
is always forever   and sister sethna
is always arranging tuberoses in a vase

do you like flowers? she asks
not particularly i tell her
my brother comes in bursting with news
india has won the test match   new zealand is wiped out

i feel like i want to pee   i tell sister sethna
my mother and my brother step out of the room
pisspot between my legs   i wait a good ten minutes
nothing happens

4 *Sponged fully. Pt has 2 small boils on lt shoulder*

a kitten has licken me limbs   so slick n clean

the curtain pulled aside
i should be able to look out the window
and see the sun
rise between the victoria terminus
and the general post office

sister levillard
is dusting my arse with talc
and my short hairs are beginning to grow again
sharply through elastoplast

om mitraya namah
om hiranyagarbhaya namah

Crabs

Look, look.
Just look at them.
The crabs.
There are two of them.

They're keeping watch.
On whom, you ask?
On you of course,
who else?

See how they're looking?
Looking at you,
naturally.
And you'll never catch them blink either.

One on this side.
One on the other.
At an angle of a hundred and sixty degrees
to your left and to your right.

They're going to eat your eyes.
That scare you?
It needn't, you know.
It's not that they're going to start eating right away.

No. But one of these days.
Tomorrow? Who knows?
If not tomorrow, then the day after.
Or ten years from now, who can tell?

They're in no hurry.
They have plenty of time.
And they can live without food
for a long time, you know.

Look this way,
quick.
Don't turn your head.
Just move your eyeballs.

Do you see a crab there?
Not the whole crab, may be,
not yet,
but you did see something move?

Now look the other way.
No, no. Not the whole head.
Just move your eyeballs
like I said.

All you can see for now
is just the pincers may be,
but you'll see,
you'll see the whole crab yet.

And you'll see it clearly.
They're only doing their job of course,
but patience
is one thing you should learn from them.

The crabs belong to you,
and to you alone.
They have no interest in eating
somebody else's eyes.

They came out of your head.
Where else do you think they came from?
But how they've grown.
Look at them now,

big fat crabs.
They've been playing a waiting game
ever since they emerged
from your head.

Malkhamb

Come climb on me.
Go right up,
all the way to the top.

Wrap yourself around me.
Crawl up and down
and all over me.

Want to trip me up?
Come on,
give it a try.

Put your arms around my neck.
Or strangle me
with your legs.

Come on, do your worst.
A thunderstorm?
Oh, I just love it!

Let's have some more of that thunder and lightning.
I want to hear it one more time.
And a little louder please, if you don't mind.

Send your thunderbolts
down
on my bald soul.

That felt good, you know.
A wig of lightning! For me?
What fun.

Have you done your worst?
And yet
here I stand,

the same as always,
unshaken
and firmly rooted to the ground

like an exercise pole in an Indian gym.
But an exercise pole
made of steel, shall we say?

Because I'm a good lightning conductor, you see.
And if nothing else,
at least I hope you had a good workout.

Old Newspapers

Beware of the old newspapers
stacked
on the little three-legged stool over there.

Don't disturb them.
I know it for a fact
that snakes have spawned in between those sheets.

Don't even look in that direction.
It's not because of the breeze
that their corners are fluttering.

It's alive, that nest of newspapers.
Newborn snakes, coiling and uncoiling,
are turning their heads to look at you.

That white corner has spread its hood.
A forked tongue
shoots out of its mouth.

Keep your eyes closed.
Get rid of the whole goddam pile if you want to
in the morning.

Buildings

A building starts to sway from side to side like an elephant.
It kneels before a gulmohur to rub its head against the bole.
It gets its tusks under the roots and begins to shake the tree.

The next one on the block to freak out is building number fourteen.
And it's catching. Number thirteen now is about to throw a fit.
Look. It has started rolling its eyes and foaming at the mouth.

All the windows are jumping. The walls are shifting. Did you notice how
Kilachand's bedroom wall just slipped away? That was smoothly done.
Patel's drawing room wall comes gliding over and slides into its place.

I think I see the chimney of Mukesh Spinning and Weaving Mill move.
The chimney of Mukesh Mill rises, it lifts clear off the ground.
Up like a pestle it goes and down it comes to pulverise the mill.

Building number eleven meanwhile is rocked by convulsions,
Like a giant epileptic battle tank in its last throes.
The penthouse on top whirls about like a gun turret.

A mighty fifty-five foot cannon is sticking out
Of Bartakke's bedroom window and it's sniffing at the horizon.

The Blanket

The blanket sprang
from the foot of the bed
and pounced on you.

It's spreading now,
spreading
all over your body.

The fringe is itching.
See
how the black fingers squirm.

A black wave breaks on your chest.
Knit, knit, the black fingers are knitting
slowly round your throat.

Feels ticklish,
doesn't it.

There's a black finger on your lips.
It's warning you
not to scream or shout for help.

Black fingers are tightening round your throat.

Wake up, man,
kick the blanket.
Strike back at it, with both feet.

Throw it off.

Or gasp
your last.

To a Cloud

I will have to describe you as an explosion of cheeks.
I'm impressed.
I cannot think of anyone else who offers such a wide range.
In all sizes and in all possible and impossible colours.
I'm not being sarcastic.
Mind? No. Why should I mind?
Two in the front and two behind
is more common,
but you can have as many cheeks as you want.
There's no rule that says that you can't.

I don't know who it belongs to –
which animal, real or imaginary,
and it could be anywhere in that jumble of cheeks –
but I'm sure there is an eye there somewhere.
And a nose too.
It's somewhere around.
Not necessarily on a face,
but then I do not know of any rule that says
that a nose always has to be in one place.

And even if there were such rules,
I'm sure they won't apply to you.
Because you're a special case.
For you, Sir Cloud,
everything is allowed.
For you, above all, are you.

You come rolling in through that window,
wiggling your arse
and smiling from cheek to cheek to cheek to cheek,
picking your nose that's sticking out of your crotch,
scratching your balls, three of them, hanging between
          your shoulder blades,
and sticking your tongue out of that arsehole in your armpit.
You come rolling in through my window

as if this room belonged to you
and you're welcome of course,
you can stay for as long as you like.
Make yourself comfortable.
But I don't have to tell you that,
do I?

All I'm saying is, on the other hand,
if you want to get the hell out,
IF I'm saying, mind you, IF you want to get the hell out,
get out of my sight and leave me alone
to study the ceiling in peace
for the rest of what remains of this night,
that's all right too.
I'm not going to stop you.
And you can get out the same way you got in you know,
in case you're wondering,
just roll out the other window!

Which, as you can see, is equally wide and equally open.
And well, ciao!
Have fun.

The Feast

Save a piece of yourself for that crow over there.
Come on crow, come and get it.
Save a piece, a tiny morsel, for that nice little sparrow.
You see her?
Come on sparrow, come and get it.
And save a piece, a titbit, for this morning's newspaper.
Any minute it will spread its wings and come for its share.

That wooden stool is not waiting for an invitation.
It will attack you like a hyena.
The radio will come charging at you
like a wild boar.
Even your old shoe will come out of hiding
with its tongue hanging out.

Hissing water pipes will come crawling out of their holes
and clothes pegs will come jumping like joyous locusts
to feast on you.

All of a sudden it will be feeding time for all things.
They will all come and crowd you and they will all be hungry.
How will you stop them?
You won't have the heart.
How will you hold them off?
Before you know it,
you'll have become
sugar
in the blood of all things.

Black Handkerchief

Blindfold yourself with a handkerchief.
A black handkerchief
if you have one.

Or an eye mask. Yes.
What could be better?
If you have a friend who works for an airline,
he could get you a nifty one.

Or why not make it at home?
Get a piece of black velvet from somewhere.
Cut a strip, about four fingers wide,
stitch a bit of tape at either end
or some elastic,

and there it is:
a homemade eye mask.
I bet your wife can make one for you
in next to no time at all.

Wrap it round your eyes
and set yourself down in an armchair,
like you were a king
sitting for a royal portrait.

You have an armchair in your house, I hope?
Oh good, you do?
That solves your problem then.

And if you can't get hold of an armchair,
not to worry.
Get a cushion.
Or even the floor will do.

Just lie down, you know.
Flat out. On your back.
And well,
just take it easy. Relax.

Not the whole time, mind you.
No, that won't do.
You will also have to go on doing whatever it is you do
to make some kind of living you know.

But as often as you can.
Every chance you get.

.

Pictures from a Marathi Alphabet Chart

Pineapple. Mother. Pants. Lemon.
Mortar. Sugarcane. Ram.
How secure they all look
each ensconced in its own separate square.

Mango. Anvil. Cup. Ganapati. Cart. House.
Medicine Bottle. Man Touching his Toes.
All very comfortable,
they all know exactly where they belong.

Spoon. Umbrella. Ship. Frock.
Watermelon. Rubberstamp. Box. Cloud. Arrow.
Each one of them seems to have found
its own special niche, a sinecure.

Sword. Inkwell. Tombstone. Longbow. Watertap.
Kite. Jackfruit. Brahmin. Duck. Maize.
Their job is just to go on being themselves
and their appointment is for life.

Yajna. Chariot. Garlic. Ostrich.
Hexagon. Rabbit. Deer. Lotus. Archer.
No, you don't have to worry.
There's going to be no trouble in this peaceable kingdom.

The mother will not pound the baby with a pestle.
The brahmin will not fry the duck in garlic.
That ship
will not crash against the watermelon.

If the ostrich won't eat the child's frock,
the archer won't shoot an arrow in Ganapati's stomach.
And as long as the ram resists the impulse,
of butting him from behind

what possible reason
could the Man–Touching–his–Toes have
to smash the cup
on the tombstone?

The One Who Did Not Go

The same old grind, day and night. I couldn't take it any more.
This time, I said to myself, I'll go to Pandharpur.

Oh, I was serious. I didn't want to be left behind.
But I saw that railway station and I quickly changed my mind.

O the sheer size of it. That's what hits you first.
My knees buckled and I was down on my arse.

I threw away my ticket. What refund, I said, I don't care.
I just want to get back home and, well, stay there.

God, I was looking forward to meeting you in the flesh,
But I'm just not cut out for travelling, I guess.

I've often wondered, do you ever come down to Bombay?
If you do, my door is always open for you, remember.

Ambu Invites Vithoba for a Round of Phugadi

Dear dear, how come you're standing alone,
all by yourself?
Aren't you going to dance? Everyone else is.
Here, give me your hands.
O come on,
this girl's going to teach you how to kick up a storm.

I know you're attached to your hands,
and your hands are attached
to your hips,
but do you think you can spare them
for just a little while
may be?

It's not as if they're of any use to you, after all,
or to anyone else for that matter.
I promise to give them back to you,
both of them.
And no one's going to make off with them either,
I assure you.

Incidentally, do you know how silly you look
just standing there?
A girl has just made you an offer of empty hands.
The offer is completely free.
But you better hurry up
because the offer's open only while the stock lasts.

You have your image to think of, I know.
And hands on hips is a great pose, I agree.
Hold it now, don't move.
Click, click, click. Thanks, I got a nice shot. Send you a copy.
But you can move now, you know.

Too many heads have rubbed against your feet,
but all the wear has been on the wrong side
or haven't you noticed?
Now and then you got to use your heels as well.

A round of phugadi will do you good.
You need some exercise.

So, what are you waiting for?
Dry your palms against that yellow silk dhoti of yours.
Stretch your palms before you,
cross them at the wrists,
hold on to my hands, real tight,

throw your body backwards, and go, man, go,
give it a whirl,
don't let go of me and you'll be all right.
And don't worry about me,
I'm an old pro at this game.

A Prostitute on a Pilgrimage to Pandharpur Visits the Photographer's Tent during the Annual Ashadhi Fair

Hey Mister, you the photographer?
I want my picture taken with Vithoba and Rakhmai.

Rakhmai to my left, Vithoba to my right
and me in the middle. That's the way I want it.

Move over Rakhmai, step aside.
Make room for me between the two of you.

Oh you're hopeless! Why are you so stiff?
They're all going to say you're a plywood god.

Come close to me, Vitthoo my dear,
and put your arm around my shoulder. There, that's better.

Rakhmai, you're jealous! But you don't have to worry.
I'll return your Vitthoo to you before I go back to Bombay.

You'll fill in some nice colours in that picture, won't you
          Mr Photographer?
Paint my sari blue and blue the body of Vitthala.

I'll take a quick look around the fair,
go for a spin in the giant wheel,

pick up a good blanket for myself,
take a peek down the Well of Death if I find the time,

and be back again in half an hour to collect my picture.
You'll keep it ready for me, won't you?

Greetings

greetings my masters
from the slave of your slave
the lowest of the low requests
permission to speak
i got news for you sir
the donkey sir
the donkey of the caste system is dead
it just collapse and die
and now its blocking the road
and getting in everyone's way
do you want to build a shrine around it?
it's already begun to rot sir
don't even go near it
it has rolled in many rubbish heaps
and has lost none of its knack for making trouble
the donkey is dead now
but that don't mean it won't kick you in the teeth
just leave it to me sir
i'll drag away the carcass
it's my job after all
you don't want its good for nothing skin do you
got a match, someone? thanks, much obliged
and where's the drummer
get him
look for him in all the gutters
douse the donkey with kerosene
i'll light it myself
hold it drummer
the moment the donkey catches fire
you can let yourself loose on the kettledrum
got it?
now
here goes

The Left Half

i'd gone to the temple the other day
but vitthala was nowhere in sight
there was just an empty brick
next to rakhmai

i shrugged and said
vitthala rakhmai what's the diff
i bowed down to her
and placed my head at her feet

withdrawing it almost immediately
you never know when
you'll need your head again
do you

but as i was leaving
i asked rakhmai casually
and where's vitthoo
don't see him around

she was surprised
vitthoo she said
isn't he standing
by my side

i looked again
just to double check
and said no
there's no one there

i've been standing here at this one spot
all my life she said
doing nothing more than looking
in front of my nose

and besides
i don't see too well
from the corners
of my eyes

and o my neck how stiff it has become
see? like a stone
i can move it neither
this way nor that

i never know about vitthoo
where he goes
when he goes or
what he's up to, nothing

i had thought vitthoo
would always be standing by my side
that's why I've been standing here
like a fool

all those people
who came here in droves
during ashadh and kartik
how come they never told me

all at once
a million years of loneliness
comes surging over me
today

Crying Mangoes in Colaba

When I was a young boy I used to go
to downtown Colaba with my father every day,
Sundays Ravivars all included,
selling fruits mangoes oranges whatever
depending on the season.
That's where my bhajan singing voice comes from incidentally,
from crying Hapoos! Paayriii! in the streets.

I'll have you picture the two of us,
father and son,
walking in and out of each other's shadows
endlessly down those kickback streets.
He a simple man with a simple pagdi on his head,
I with a huge and rather ostentatious basket on mine,
practically staggering under its weight,
he with a pair of down to earth chappals on his feet,
I with calluses dust or mudboots on mine,
depending on my whim
the time of year or the dictates of fashion.

Once our walk had taken us further than
we usually went, way past the military barrier, when
my father stopped and said Let's call it a day,
we haven't sold a thing today but it's getting late.
We were about to turn around and head for home
when we saw five soldiers, Brits, coming our way.
O good, I thought, customers, but I was wrong.
They surrounded me, I could feel
the basket emptying rapidly over my head,
and the next minute they were gone.
This was fine by me except for the fact
that they hadn't bothered to pay.
I had not realised it until then
that the weight of an empty basket
can be much more than a full one sometimes.
And they had been good mangoes too,
handpicked Alphonsoes all, of the finest quality,
that's what really pissed my father off.

As it happened, my father knew a lawyer, a biggie, which helped,
how else would hicks like us have got
within earshot of the army brass?
The big man in khaki heard my father out and said
Will you be able to identify the men?
My father, simple man that he was, looked doubtful and said
That may be difficult.
O but I can, I said, hastily butting in.
The big man, a Brit of course,
looked approvingly at me and said Good boy
I'll line them all up in front of you then.
You just point them out to me, the thieving bastards.

White men you know they all look the same to me
but all the same I walked past them
with a straight face and narrowed eyes,
examining each fat and fruity face closely.
They all appeared about equally ripe for the knife
and each one seemed to say to me Please, Balwant, spare me,
but finally it had to be done. I picked
five of them at random you may say,
pointing a finger as I said Him
and him and him and him and uh... was it him or him?
Let me see now. No doubt about it, it was him.

A random choice I agree and no not fair at all
but have a heart.
How was a poor boy like me to produce
five real thieves
in a world that's getting more unreal by the day?
We got our money back didn't we?
Fifty bucks from five different pockets.
Recovering money, I tell you,
is the biggest headache in this line of business.

A Highly Prejudiced Account of a Bhajan Session that took place in 1921 or thereabouts in the Office of Patrick Kelly, the then Police Commissioner of Bombay, at which Govindbua Presented a Marathi Song Written by Dnyaneshwar in the 13th century

Govindbua, you've got to be some kind of a genius.
The way you tortured that innocent song
in the police commissioner's office the other day,
I don't think I'll ever completely recover from
the circus band treatment you gave it.
But then, like it says in the song:
That Vitthala is good, O that Madhava is good.

The whole farce took place in front of Kelly Sahib.
And who do you think was on the harmonium?
Appropriately enough, Atmaram the butcher.
The man should've been arrested on the spot.
Will no one even try to rescue that poor harmonium?
But then, what does the song say:
That Vitthala is good, O that Madhava is good.

Vitthal Munde's got a crick in the neck.
Where was the need to nod his head
with such ecstatic approval
every time Govindbua unleashed a taan
that can only be described as, well, European?
But never mind. Like the song has it:
That Vitthala is good, O that Madhava is good.

The man doesn't know his treble from his bass.
He really slaughtered the harmonium that day.
Illegally, too; have you ever heard
all the seven notes going 'Ba... Ba...' at the same time?
It's still not too late to hang him I say.
But then, as the song would have it:
That Vitthala is good, O that Madhava is good.

Don't tell me, Govindbua; let me guess:
It's a rubber taal and a fuckall raag; right?
To sing the way you do, round and about all notes,
without hitting a single one even accidentally
has to be some kind of an achievement.
But then, how does the song go:
That Vitthala is good, O that Madhava is good.

Stop that song, says George the Fifth, suing for peace.
Stop that song, and you can have your bloody swaraj.
Your prickly fifth is making my beard itch like mad.
Will someone be good enough
to scratch his majesty's beard please?
Don't you know what the song says:
That Vitthala is good, O that Madhava is good.

That was fantastic, said Kelly Sahib to Govindbua.
I think you're the greatest bhajan singer of all time.
In fact, I'll give it to you in writing.
A proper certificate.
Will you come back and pick it up from my secretary tomorrow?
Or, in the words of the song itself:
That Vitthala is good, O that Madhava is good.

Now that he has a certificate to prove it,
the man has really started believing in all that crap
about him being a genius and god knows what else.
He actually carries that thing on his person at all times,
and is ever ready to flash it before everyone he meets.
And why not? The song says:
That Vitthala is good, O that Madhava is good.

By now they've begun to dread the sight of Govindbua
from Mandvi to Worli,
and the sight of the short and curly signature
of Sir Patrick Kelly.
Well well well well well well well, says Balwantbua.
But the song says it all:
That Vitthala is good, O that Madhava is good.

A Song for Yalloo

Hurry up, Yalloo, run along,
your seth's on his way up.
You'd better go, dear girl,
and meet him halfway down the stairs.

They say he was a famous lawyer once,
but look at him now, the poor man,
both feet planted on the first step
– he can barely stand.

He looks up at the steps
that rise steeply before him.
The staircase is in session,
the court of last appeal.

How old is he now? Eighty, at least.
Lead him up gently, Yalloo.
Careful now... we're nearly there...
Made it!

Aren't you going to take
that parcel from his hands?
What has he brought for you this time,
I wonder. Something nice, I bet.

Make him comfortable in bed now,
surround him with pillows.
You'll have to untie
his dhoti for him, I'm afraid.

Then both of you can take your time
painting each other's fingernails.
Remove the comb from his pocket
and give it to him.

The man likes nothing better than
combing your beautiful hair.
And why not if it makes him happy.
You just sit still, and let him.

How much of an appetite
do you think a man has, at his age?
Looks like he just wants
to pamper you a bit.

The best part is he'll be
no trouble at all in bed.
He'll just hold you close
and lie down for half an hour or so,

with all the passion of a sick man
lying on his side,
clutching a hot water bottle
in a slack embrace.

There's nothing of that in him.
After all these years,
in this strange lover of yours, perhaps
you've found the father you never had.

So hurry up, Yalloo, run along,
your seth's on his way up.
I'm sure he's going to leave
his entire estate to you, and to you alone.

Chirimiri

How automatically your hand
slips into your pocket
when you see a policeman.

Is there someone still out there
who does not take a bribe?
They talk about Yama,
but even he belongs to the same tribe.

So why try to run or hide under your bed?
You don't have to.
Next time you see him coming
try a little cash instead.

Why try yoga, visit holy places
or go to the spiritual gym,
when it's so much simpler just to toss
god's shining name like a coin at him?

After all your only crime
is that you were born.
Just say you're sorry, you won't do it again,
and may be he'll let you off this time.

If I were to die,
they'll all say What a disgrace.
If that's what he wanted to do in the end,
why was the fucker born in the first place!

I think it's a shame.
Why should a citizen of India
have to be born again and again?

Of course you can try to fool him
with a false moustache,
but next time you see him coming
try a bit of cash.

Gently smoothen the crumpled name of god
in the hollow of his palm,
fold it thrice
and tell him to get lost.

To die? For what? To be born again?
Forget it, says Balwantbua.
If there's one thing I hate it's to repeat myself.

III Words for Music

Tape Me Drunk

tape me drunk
my sister
my chipmunk

don't tie me down
promise me pet
don't tie me down
to a hospital bed

my salvation i believe
is in a basket of broken eggs
yolk on my sleeve
and vomit on my legs

o world
what is my worth
o streets
where is my shirt

begone my psychiatrist
boo
but before you do
just take off your pants
and leave them behind

i don't need you
i know i've pissed in mine
but there's nothing wrong
with my mind

Third Pasta Lane Breakdown

nothing's wrong with me   man   i'm ok
it's just that i haven't had a drink all day

let me finish my first glass of beer
and this shakiness will disappear

you'll have to light my cigarette i can't strike a match
but see the difference once the first drink's down the hatch

after a drink you ask me to test fly a jet
i'll take it up and fill the sky with figures of eight

from taxi to speakeasy is a long way to go
let me hold on to you i'll need your support

from taxi to speakeasy every step i take
is like doing a tightrope during an earthquake

nothing's wrong with me a drink won't cure
my hand will be steady as a rock   my step will be sure

put me on a stretcher   it's an emergency
rush me to the nearest speakeasy

let me lie down in the middle of the road
go get a bottle of hooch and pour it down my throat

Door to Door Blues

it's only eleven   were you asleep   o well
at least i didn't ring the wrong doorbell

thank god i found your place   i been here before
but it's dark outside   one can't see the name on the door

i was wondering if you'd let me stay the night
i haven't eaten all day   i could do with a bite

a slice of bread will do or maybe a sausage
then i'll lie down in the balcony or here in the passage

i won't be trouble i'm used to sleeping on the floor
please don't bother i don't want a blanket don't want a pillow

i'm completely broke i've nowhere else to go
i can't sleep on the road   the cops have told me so

you won't have to ask me to join you for breakfast tomorrow
i'll answer the door when the milkman comes and i will go

Taxi Song

i been checking out on my friends
and it looks like i've none
they know i'm down on luck
they know i'm on a drunk
they know i'll come ask for money
and so they hide or run

up and down and round about
from one end of town to the other
you taken me to ten addresses
from colaba to dadar
you think i aint gonna pay you
after all that trouble
well that's where you are wrong
'cause I'm gonna pay you double

so don't stop now
taxi driver
don't stop now and please don't shout
i'm not gonna pay you now
and you aint gonna throw me out
i know i've run up quite a bill
but take me to this place on malabar hill
and i'll pay you double like i said i will

i got a friend he stays on malabar hill
in a place that's got a swimming pool
i've known him since we were in school
we shared a desk in class
the same girl gave us the clap
and if i remember right
he still owes me 27 bottle caps

i do hope he is in town
'cause he will never let me down
there is a chance and if it clicks
he'll gimme a couple of hundred chips
we'll go some place and have a drink
find ourselves a couple of chicks

we gonna have a lotta fun together
what do you say
but i'll insist on just one thing
you must let me pay

so can the curses
switch off the shouting
it aint getting us anywhere
we can sit and talk till break of day
and i'll still have no money to pay the fare
so let's try something new man
let's get a move on

Nobody

you slept on a railway platform 3 days in a row
you haven't changed your shirt you let your beard grow
you ring a bell the door opens just a crack
you phone a friend you're told he'll call you back
nobody wants to see you and that's a fact

you tell your friend that he's a bastard and a liar
he pretends not to hear he just swivels in his chair
shankar's having trouble with income tax
alimony is breaking kooji's back
nobody wants to lend you money and that's a fact

where your next drink's coming from's what you would like to know
your bootlegger stopped giving you credit a long time ago
the receptionist seems not to notice your collar is black
but g m's out of town she doesn't know when he'll be back
nobody wants to give you a job and that's a fact

the lift is out of order and you know it for sure
that you will never make it to the ground floor
you begin to shake at the head of the stairs you get an attack
put your foot forward but quickly draw it back
they all think you're already at the bottom and that's a fact

Hi Constable

hi constable   tell me what's your collar size
same as mine   i bet this shirt will fit you right

the shirt is yours   feel it   don't you like the fall
all you got to do to get it is one phone call

here's the number   two nine four three seven nine
write it down   my friend will come and pay the fine

the pig who picked me up last night and brought me in
has to be the one who licked my wallet clean

the pig who booked me under clause hundred and ten
was the one who took my wristwatch and my pen

i've nothing left to give you you can take my shirt
a little soiled but it's new under the dirt

you tell me i hit a policeman on the chin
for my part i don't know if i did or didn't

you say i unzipped my fly and pissed on his desk
when the inspector asked my name and permanent address

yes if what you say is even halfway true
a week in jail i know might even do me good

yes i know i fully deserve what's coming to me
please but don't you see this time i've got to be free

Cold Stone Sober

cold stone sober
on a cold stone floor
you wake up in a lock up
you're blacked out and shook up
you don't know where you are
and you don't know how you got there
you have a catch in your neck
you have a match in your hair
your back is sore
from sleeping on the floor
you can see in the dark
you're surrounded by bars

you don't know what's the time
you don't know what's the crime
you got ants in your pants
you badly want to pee
the window is on high
it shows a black sky
you pull yourself up
on level with the sill

all you get to see
is the top of a tree
you look in your pockets
you find your money gone
you don't know what you done
you wonder where's the john
what did you steal
who did you kill
you pick your way
through ankles and elbows
you stand on your toes
in a pool of urine
you hope it's all a dream
you look around
find a cigarette on the ground
it's only a stub

but you pick it up
will the cop have a light
why not ask he might
he throws you a match
but you're a bad catch

A Fraction of a Second before the Action Starts

a fraction of a second before the action starts
just before the blind lane spills its guts of glass
how do you see your role my friend in the final reel
what's that in your hand – a stone or a steering wheel
think my friend for your own sake
think there will be just one take
which side of the windscreen will you be on
in the year of twisted metal and the flying stone

just before the shops get sick and spoil the streets
and throw up tv sets and bras at your feet
how do you see your role my friend in the final reel
are your hands free – you'll need them both to steal
hey but perhaps that's you mister
come out from behind the cash register
which side of the counter will you be on
in the year of twisted metal and the flying stone

here's the script my friends underline your parts
study it carefully before the action starts
we'll skip the camera – so you'll feel
less self conscious – yeah we'll make it real
all the same there will be shooting
and now the action can begin
which side of the gun will you be on
in the year of twisted metal and the flying stone

Spinach for Dinner

whenever something happens
i mean something really bad
like you fail in your exams
and don't know how to tell your dad
i don't know why it is
but there is always spinach for dinner

whenever something happens
whenever things look pretty black
your girl marries the other guy
or your boss gives you the sack
you come home that night
and find that there's spinach for dinner

you wander around all day
wondering how rat poison will taste
because your girlfriend's gonna marry
the pilot from kuwait
you get home late and find
there indeed is spinach for dinner

you feel like the roof caved in
you're surrounded by the rubble
you keep your cool you shrug off a beam
remove a tile from the dinner table
you don't have to look
it has to be spinach for dinner

Been Working on this Statue

been working on this statue for close to forty years
it's getting nowhere it's only going from bad to worse
an uncooperative half ton of modeling clay
has settled in my bathtub and refuses to go away
i keep it covered in yards of wet jacquard
and hang around its neck a don't touch placard
i inaugurate a trade fair pat a child on the head address
a meeting but i always return to my work in progress

been working on this statue for close to forty years
it aint coming right it's only going from bad to worse
a human figure it isn't yet but that's what i had planned
a human figure a nude a man his cock in his hand
a statue of a man his measurements same as mine
except that i'd like to make him a wee bit taller than i'm
i also expect to make him broader shouldered than i'm
my tailor's written saying he wouldn't mind

been working on this statute for close to forty years
it aint coming right it's only going from bad to worse
i peel off a cheek to give some substance to his calf
or to deepen his chest but it only makes him laugh
i knock off a toe or gouge out an eye
to give him a proper nose or to propitiate his thigh
i pluck his ear to give him a lump in the throat
and i'll go to the supreme court to give him his right to vote

been working on this statue for close to forty years
it aint coming right it's only going from bad to worse
i always meant to cast it in bronze and give it to the state
the state may well decide to put it up in front of india gate
or maybe he'll be carried coast to coast in a mobile van
on display for the benefit of one and all in this poor land
or maybe bury it in a pyramid along with my embalmed body
with all my concubines eunuchs wives and pots of toddy

been working on this statue for close to forty years
it's going from bad to worse and now i'm close to tears
to lug it from bathroom to garage is itself gonna be a job
but i'll have to drag the tub to my car and get it to the top
i'll find a rope and tie the damn thing to the top of my jalopy
i'll go for a drive to the pier i'll drive right on into the sea
yeah we'll go for a ride the two of us just me and him
we'll find out what's what and who's who for one of us can swim

I Saw a Hair Growing

i saw a hair growing in my toilet soap
i pulled it out and placed it under a microscope

it curled and kicked the fat lens it happened kind of fast
but it did somehow get under the skin of glass

i ran a razor over the potbellied lens
it grew again magnified ten thousand times

i smashed the microscope with the blow of a sledgehammer
i hurled insults at the hair but it could only stammer

the hair stood before me my equal in height
and the hair said stand up like a man and fight

the hair snarled and said stand up like a man and fight
the hair lashed out at me and i went out like a light

What's a Man to Do if a Well Runs Dry

what's a man to do if a well runs dry
sink another where the water is high

your divining rod will get a start
that's not when you stop your bullock cart

your divining rod will begin to twitch
keep cool   that's not where to dig a ditch

your divining rod will stand on end
stop now this is where you camp my friend

there's good grass around god be praised
unhitch the cart   let the bullocks graze

unpack the pick   the shovel   the drill   the lot
or dig with bare hands if that's all you got

manufacturers will be happy to send
a catalogue if you want the equipment

chop the cart and start a fire nice and warm
where's your ballpoint   fill in this order form

you'll have to wait awhile   how do you feel
if the fire's dying out add a wheel

meanwhile if you're thirsty all you do
is pierce a bullock's neck with a corkscrew

be sure to seal the puncture with band-aid
after a drink of blood and before the bullock's dead

eat your dog and don't let him eat you
don't give him blood though a dog gets thirsty too

Molotov Cocktail

finish your drink
and give me that empty bottle of gin
come now my friends
the real fun's about to begin
i want that champagne bottle
when its empty
i want to put some real life
into this party
i'll have the empties
you have the scotch
i'll show you how to mix
a molotov cocktail watch

you've played your party games
you've had your fun
but i bet my friends
you haven't heard this one
molotov cocktail
is the name of the game you fools
and as we go along
i'll explain the rules
can you make a molotov cocktail
i'll show you how
i'll give you a demonstration
i mean now

your gardener will get some earth
in this casserole
ask the driver to go
get a can of petrol
fill a third of the bottle with earth
the rest with gas
leave a hole in the cork
so the fuse can pass
i like that lighter of yours
slide it across the carpet
i'll be damned   it's gold
thanks   i think i'll keep it

attention everybody
attention
i'm about to give you
a demonstration
the party is over
a great good time was had by all
now do as i tell you
you   and you there   up against the wall
i just want to see your bodies fall
and hit the ground
i want to see your bodies fall
with strobes around

ah the lighter works
now put your fingers in your ears
wait for the explosion
here goes bang and cheers

Joe and Bongo Bongo

joe and bongo bongo
have moved to their new home
with sunken baths and running water
hot and cold

a home that cost the zoo
fifteen thousand pounds
the zoo hopes a home where boredom is
out of bounds

the co-director of the zoo
miss sarah evans said
the gorillas will have a colour
tv set

miss sarah evans said
in a press release
we want nothing but happiness
for the gorillas

wild wallpaper and drapes
repeat the baobab motif
that pongos pay no rent is the best
part of it

gorillas dig sci-fi
and lap up commercials
while munching lots of nuts and assorted
roots and bulbs

joe dreamed he shot the sheriff
right through the tin star
and went across to have a drink
into the bar

just then bongo bongo
interrupted the programme
to say a few nice words about a
dental cream

Radio Message from a Quake Hit Town

please send help
please send help urgently
walls are coming together
as if giant hands were closing in

everything is destroyed
everything
please send help
please send a helicopter
the centre of town is under water
everyone thinks only
of his own family

please send help
please send help urgently
isn't it a pity
the authorities in lima
don't realise how serious
the situation is

the rescue plane
flies over the town
and all the pilot can see
is a cloud of dust

Poor Man

i'm a poor man from a poor land and everything about me is wrong
my guitar is warped my voice cracks but i've written a damned good song

i'm a poor man from a poor land my ma is blind and so is my dad
my one sister is dumb the other is seven and my elder brother is mad

i'm a poor man from a poor land and i play a poor guitar
but don't you think i have the right to be a superstar

i'm a poor man from a poor land and i'll change my name and grow a mane
if that's gonna be of any help if i don't die rich i'll die insane

i'm a poor man from a poor land and i know it makes no sense at all
but i want a villa in the south of france and i want a gold disk on my wall

i'm a poor man from a poor land let me pass my hat around
it's much too big for one man's head but i need your dollars and pounds

i'm a poor man from a poor land my ma is blind and so is my dad
my one sister is dumb the other is seven and of course my english is bad

i'm a poor man from a poor land my age ain't right my colour is wrong
my nose too big my chest too small my arm too long my grip too strong

i'm a poor man from a poor land i've got together a naked band
of hungry poets with woodcut ribs hey what chance do you think i stand

i'm a poor man from a poor land brother can you spare a dime
got no father got no mother or did i tell you that they was blind

i'm a poor man from a poor land and i'm sure you'll like my pitch
put me on top of every chart buy this record and make me rich

IV Translations

if death's

NAMDEO

if death's
about to pounce
we'll sing
we'll dance

what song
suits which hour
o lord
i've no idea

cymbals and drums
beat thisaway
and my song
goes thataway

     nama says:

don't you ever
give me the sack
not in this life
nor in those to come

in the beginning

NAMDEO

in the beginning
is the ant
mouth of the triple river
is the mouth of the ant

in darkness
is the ant
in flames a wick of water
lights a lamp of soot

in the wake
of the ant
all the sky follows

the world of our making's her dropping

i pursue
that ant
i, visnudas nama
unlock the ant with my guru

i eat god

JANABAI

i eat god
i drink god
i sleep
on god

i buy god
i count god
i deal
with god

god is here
god is there
void is not
devoid of god

    jani says:

god is within
god is without
and moreover
there's god to spare

see the void
JANABAI

see the void
above the void
on its top
another void

the first void
is red
it's called
the lower void

the higher void
is white
the middle void
is grey

but the great void
is blue
it contains
only itself

jani was struck
with wonder
when she heard
the silent bell

god my darling

JANABAI

god my darling
do me a favour and kill my mother-in-law

i will feel lonely when she is gone
but you will be a good god won't you
and kill my father-in-law

i will be glad when he is gone
but you will be a good god won't you
and kill my sister-in-law

i will be free when she is gone
i will pick up my begging bowl
and be on my way

let them drop dead says jani
then we will be left alone
just you and me

the zoom ant

MUKTABAI

the zoom ant
swallowed the sun
the barren woman
begot a son

a scorpion went
to the lower depths
shesha bowed to him
with a thousand heads

a pregnant fly
delivered a kite
having seen it all
mukta smiled

wonder of wonders

EKNATH

wonder of wonders
a thief stole a town
but when the trackers tracked him down
no thief, no town

the town was entirely unfounded
the temple windblown
god confounded
the steeple shot across heaven

the foundation fled
to the recesses of hell
and the wall wandered
from door to door

the foundation the wall the temple
underneath all paradox
the meaning is simple

Who cares for God's man?

TUKARAM

Who cares for God's man?
No one but God himself.

Cousin or companion to no one,
He's beyond reclamation.

They call him idle, a madman.
He becomes a problem for everyone.

Forsaken by the last human being,
He's usually found in deserted places.

After bathing he smears ash on himself.
People criticise him.

With a rosary round his neck he sits apart.
They say, What's the matter with the bastard?

Any time and any place suits his song.
His father, his mother, his brother, they curse him.

How did any woman beget him? his wife wonders.
Why, I wish the eunuch were dead.

He renounces the world he's heir to;
That's why, O my cowherds, he's so special.

He, declares Tuka, is the end of the way,
Who chucks up the world.

Lesser

TUKARAM

Lesser
Than a molecule
Tuka is like the
Sky in magnitude.

His own cadaver
And world-wonder
He has eaten
And excreted.

He's absolved
Of triputi.
A flame has begun in
His earthen lamp.

Now, says Tuka,
If I live on
I only
Outlive myself.

I'm tied to this

TUKARAM

I'm tied to this
Sword and this
Shield, said the knight.
How can I fight?

How do you suppose
A man fights or flees
With a whole horse
Between his knees?

My armour my helmet
Are allies of death,
Insists the wretch
Beset with assets.

    Tuka says:

Man is the great
Brahma in person but
The fool disregards
The footprints of saints.

My body takes on

TUKARAM

My body takes on
A cadaverous aspect
And I find my way
To the burning-ghat.

Desire, anger, love
Weep unceasingly.
Codes of conduct wail,
Disconsolate.

The dung cakes of
Vairagya press
Against my limbs.
The apocalypse flares.

Smashed, the earthen pot
Spills embers at
My feet. Mourners toll
The sky like a bell.

I disown my lineage,
My name, my mien.
I restore my body
To whom it belongs.

Now all is well and
Effortlessly ash.
The guru graced the lamp
With a flame, says Tuka.

Don't think I don't

TUKARAM

Don't think I don't
Know you, you swine,
My born enemy, you
Married me by design.

Is this humiliation
To last forever?
Am I to seek charity
For my daily bread and butter?

What I want
To know is
What good has he done
The two of us?

The woman's in tears,
Says Tuka, she sobs,
Then she laughs
And then again sobs.

What now my son

TUKARAM

What now my son,
What will you eat?
Your old man's become
God's idiot.

He has given up
All pretence of trade.
In penitent fury
He batters his forehead.

Wears all kinds of
Funny beads; worries
Only about himself.
We don't matter.

Castanets get the jitters
When he opens
His ugly mouth
To sing in the temple.

He would rather be in
The jungle; home
Has little use for him.
What do we do now?

Don't get excited, woman,
Tuka says.
This is only
The beginning.

We are the enduring bums

TUKARAM

We are the enduring bums.
Thieves regard us with consternation.
When we go out and beg
Dogs manage our households.

Get lost, brother, if you don't
Fancy our kind of living.
There's no better way
Of growing to greatness of soul.

With great perseverance
We've built us a timeless shack,
Delicate as the wood of castor,
Shy even of its weight.

Every home is our bank
And granary.
If food is ours for the asking
Why bother with animal husbandry.

Our security is complete.
Cow dung and mud is our capital.
In coats of cow dung and mud
Our walls shine.

God, says Tuka, has rid us
Of all envy.
And God again
Looks after our families.

I followed

TUKARAM

I followed
No manuals of mukti.
Never cared about
Penance and such.

Help! I hollered
From where I lay.
God, get me out of
This hole.

Didn't bring holy water
For your bath, did I?
Meditation is all
The service I offered.

A lot of words
Flaked off Tuka.
With uncritical grace
You accepted them.

Narayan

TUKARAM

Narayan
Is insolvent.
He has borrowed
Right and left.

Pay up, pay up,
Clamour the creditors.
He dare not stir
In his own house.

He hides
Under the bed.
Maya declares
He isn't in.

I don't make
A lot of noise
As the debt is old,
Old as the world.

See the note
He signed,
With the four Vedas
As witnesses.

Tuka the shopkeeper
The said creditor...
Vithal
The said debtor...

Magnified in every direction
TUKARAM

Magnified in every direction
I'm a monstrosity

My body leaves out nothing
Is never the same

I like my new job, my new boss
I'm no more the beast of burden

But the luckiest donkey in the world
Nothing weighs on my mind or body

Space is more spacious than ever
Without a direction to follow

I stretch myself in the courtyard of saints
Abandoned by the last louse

Power has spoilt Tuka
He has become extremely intolerant

Tuka has it made, he struts about
Flamboyantly caparisoned

Believe me, saints

TUKARAM

Believe me, saints,
I'm really no good.
I'm worthy neither
Of respect nor love.

I know what I'm saying;
I didn't get anywhere.
They think highly of me
Because others do.

Plagued by life,
I took to herding cattle,
Until exhausted by both
I decided to give up.

I didn't have to distribute
My wealth among brahmins
As whatever money there was
I'd lost it all.

I became a wretched beggar,
Abandoning
My brother, my child,
And the woman I loved.

Hating to be seen, I wandered
Through the jungle, sought
The cave. I never elected
My own company.

Tuka's devotion
Is of no great import.
With him it's merely
A family tradition.

There's no percentage

TUKARAM

There's no percentage
In being renowned
When our dialogue
Brings no dividends.

As far as I'm concerned,
God doesn't exist.
I'm starving; cut out
The dinner table jokes.

I garnished my tongue
With a lot of language,
But was farthest
From any feeling.

An emigrant now, I'm
A citizen of No Land;
I gave up sansara
Without gaining you.

If only I'd known,
Says Tuka,
I'd have desisted
From such folly.

It was a case

TUKARAM

It was a case
Of God rob God.
No cleaner job
Was ever done.

God left God
Without a bean.
God left no trace
No trail no track.

The thief was lying
Low in His flat.
When he moved
He moved fast.

    Tuka says:
Nobody was
Nowhere. None
Was plundered
And lost nothing.

You pawned

TUKARAM

You pawned
Your feet
And got
My faith.

Love is
The interest:
I say
Shell out.

Your name
Is my document
– And your funeral.
Listen

    Says Tuka:

You who make
The eagle manifest –
My guru will be
My witness.

I it was

TUKARAM

I it was
Begat me.
My knees
Received me.

My one desire
Granted,
Of all desire
I'm deserted.

A new power
Moves me
Since that hour
Killed me.

Look at him
Either way;
Tuka is the same
As always.

Tuka tiptoed

TUKARAM

Tuka tiptoed
Back home
Leaving God
In his temple.

The sidekick knew
That boss would
Want him to do
Just that.

When on a timeless bed
God relaxes,
It isn't well-bred
To hang around.

Better go home,
Tuka tells everyone.
Don't disturb him,
He's asleep.

Blasted

TUKARAM

Blasted,
The seed is popcorn.
Birth and death
Both we scorn.

Form
Is out of place.
God we have
Figured in the flesh.

Sugar transcends
The sugarcane.
We bypass the womb
And the pain.

All, says Tuka,
Is only apparent.
And everybody
Is Pandurang.

Tuka is stark raving mad

TUKARAM

Tuka is stark raving mad
He talks too much

His vocabulary:
Ram Krishna Govind Hari

Of any God save Pandurang
Tuka is ignorant

He expects revelation
At any time, from any one

Words on him are wasted
He dances before God, naked

Weary of men and manners
With pleasure he rolls in gutters

Ignoring instruction, all
He ever says is 'Vithal, Vithal'

O pundits, O learned ones
Spit him out at once

I've had my days

TUKARAM

I've had my days.
Good. Bad.
Now my strength
Leaves me.

Now I cannot
Move about.
I'm empty.
Empty and hollow.

I retain my
Lineaments
Like a charred
Cloth its creases.

I'm insubstantial
Says Tuka;
Ash to the touch
Of the world.

Lacking the guile

TUKARAM

Of a mass hypnotiser
I merely extol your name
And sing your praises
Not being a miracle worker

Or a faith healer
Without a train
Of disciples to boast of
Being the patriarch

Of no monastery
But a mere
Shopkeeper
No high priest or seer

No necromancer
No exorcist
No witchdoctor
Lacking the guile

Neither the storyteller
With a grand narrative style
Nor the wretched pundit
Stewed in dialectics

Not a fool
Among fools
Wagging
A sage beard

There's no voodoo about Tuka
Tuka is like
None of these
Hell-begotten lunatics

Without seeing a thing

TUKARAM

Without seeing a thing
I've seen entirely.
I've achieved a likeness
Of everybody.

Without taking
I've accepted.
My arms and legs
Are holidays.

Without eating
I've had my fill.
My mouth as it watered
Became the menu.

Without a word
I've spoken.
I've presented what
At best was absent.

The poem occurs,
Says Tuka,
Unknown
To my ears.

What will I eat now

TUKARAM

What will I eat now,
Where will I go?
Do I dare to stay on
In the village?

The villagers furious,
Their chieftain grumpy,
If I beg I'll only see
The door in my face.

I'm shameless, they say,
An exhibitionist.
The elders in a conference
Are taking a decision.

The angry gentry
Have done their bit
And brought ruin
On a defenceless man.

What do I want, says Tuka,
With these people?
I must get going now
And search for Vithal.

Harvest Done

TUKARAM

Harvest done,
Good times ahead.
Now's time our own
To lose in love.

From everything
Is freedom.
Fatigue is not
Any more.

How singular Pandurang
Are all things!
The world belongs
To no one in particular.

We are all
Bejewelled, bespangled.
Each one of us sparkles
Like a jewel on the other.

We serve, says Tuka,
The great all timer
And none else if any
There be besides.

V   the boatride

the long hooked poles
know the nooks and crannies
find flaws in stonework
or grappling with granite
ignite a flutter
of unexpected pigeons
and the boat is jockeyed away from
the landing

after a pair of knees
has shot up and streaked
down the mast after
the confusion of hands about
the rigging

an off white miracle

the sail
      spreads

    *

because a sailor waved
                    back
to a boy
          another boy
      waves to another sailor

in the clarity of air
the gesture withers for want
of correspondence and
the hand that returns to him
the hand his knee accepts
as his own
         is the hand
of an aged person
            a hand
that must remain patient
and give the boy it's a part of
time
    to catch up

    *

frozen in a suit the foreman
self-conscious beside
his more self-conscious spouse
finds illegible the palm that opens
demandingly before him

the mould of his hands
broken about his right knee
he reaches for a plastic wallet
and pays the fares

along the rim of the boat
lightly the man rests his arm
without brushing against
his woman's shoulder

                gold
and sunlight
           fight
for the possession of her throat
when she shifts
in the wooden seat

and the newly weds exchange
smiles for small profit

    *

show me a foreman he says
to himself
        who knows
his centreless grinding
oilfired saltbath furnace better
than i do
      and swears
at the seagull
who invents
on the spur of the air
what is clearly the whitest inflection
known
      and what is
clearly for the seagull

over and above the waves
a matter of course

      *

the speedboat swerves off
leaving behind a divergence of sea
and the whole harbour all
that floats must bear
the briny brunt
the sailboat
hurls its hulk over
burly rollers
surmounted soon in leaps
and bounds

a gull hitched on hump
the long trail toils on
bringing to every craft
a measure of imbalance
a jolt for a dingy
a fillip to a schooner
a swagger to a ketch

and after the sea wall
scabby and vicious with shells
has scalped the surge
after the backwash
has reverted to the bulk of water
all things that float
resume
a normal vacillation

      *

winds bargaining over
his shrunken head
the mousy patriarch overgrown
with grandchildren
classifies a ship
first asserts and then proves
to the newest generation

that sea water
is salty
with the authority
of age *you'll get*
he tells the youngest
wet
    so putting in a nutshell
the dire consequence
of falling in water

the child cogitates
while the eyes of his
contemporaries
are already riveted
proudly to the portuguese ship they learn
the indians captured

     *

his wife has dismissed
the waves like a queen
a band of oiled
acrobats

if her shuttered eyes
move in dark circles
they move against her will

winds
like the fingers
of an archaeologist
move across her stony face
and across the worn
edict of a smile
cut thereon

her husband in chains
is brought before her
he clanks and grovels

throw him to the wolves
she says

staring fixedly
at a hair in his right nostril

      *

impatient with the surrounding gallons
of boredom spurning the rowdy
intangibles of waves
a two year old renounces
his mother's ear
and begins to cascade
down her person
rejecting her tattooed arm
denying her thighs
undaunted by her knees
and further down
her shanks
devolving
         he demands
              balloons
                  and balloons
from father to son
          are handed
          down

closer to keel than all
elders are
and down there
honoured among boots
chappals and bare feet
he goes into a huddle with
               the balloons
               coming to grips

with one
      being persuasive
with another
      and setting an example
      by punishing a third

      *

two sisters
that came
last
when the boat
nearly started

seated side
by side
athwart
on a plank
have not
spoken

hands in lap
they have
been looking
past the boatman's
profile

splicing
the wrinkles
of his saline
face

and loose ends
of the sea

      *

familiar perspectives
reoccupy
a cleanlier eye
sad as a century
the gateway of india
struggles back to its feet
wobbly but sober enough
to account for itself
details approach our memory
ingratiatingly
we are prepared to welcome
a more realistic sense
of proportion

a wind comes carrying
                    the microbe
of a melody

where the sea jostles
against the wall
vacuous sailboats snuggle
tall and gawky
their masts at variance
    islam
            mary
                    dolphin

their names appearing
                    music

a black back turned
on all the waters of the arabic sea
a man plays on a bulbul tarang
alone on the last boat
and facing the wall

        *

the boat courses around
to sidle up
against the landing

the wall sweeps by
magisterially
superseding
the music man

an expanse of
unswerving stone
encrusted coarsely
with shells
admonishes our sight

Appendices

I Poems

an alphabet for darshan

a is for alligator
naturally naturally
a is for arun
legally legally
a is for alfalfa
greedily greedily
a is for z
gradually gradually

b is for bells on her toes
b is for a bargain of verbs
like bulldoze bamboozle befuddle
b is for button button
b is for buttocks
alternately alternately

c is for chhabdas
grossly grossly
c is for copywriting
bravely bravely
c is for codopyrin
perversely perversely
c is for cockroach
kill it kill it

d is for dear darling darshan
d is for duck dubuck duck
d is for dysentery
rudely rudely
d is for the dense dark tree

e is for eliot
classically classically
e is for ellis bridge
elsewherely
e is for e-honey

sweetly sweetly
e is for eddy duchin
reciprocally

f is for fuddy duddy
f is for fa fae fo fum
f is for fol de rol de rolly o
f is for the fever in the bone

g is for gargling
gloriously gloriously
g is for glendora
freely freely
g is for GO TO HELL
h is for hopstepjumpkins
breathlessly

h is for hercule poirot
inadequately
h is for the henpecked hubby
h is for ha ha

i is for irate wife kills husband
i is for insomnia
verily verily
i is for i'll make water
i is for you
annually annually

j is for jack
tumblingly tumblingly
j is for jill
similarly similarly
j is for justice the justice
j is for ja jaa

k is for kolatkars
witheringly witheringly
k is for kotex
comfortably comfortably
k is for kauphy
wrongly wrongly

l is for love love love love love love
l is for lollypops
lingeringly lingeringly
l is for limejuice with daddy
l is for lumumba
obviously obviously

m is for mistakes
innumerably innumerably
m is for moog dal
merely merely
m is for mosquitoes
unmistakably
m is for the men you meet in lifts

n is for never
repeatedly repeatedly
n is for *nahi tar kai*
n is for nylon nighty
clearly clearly
n is for nothing doing

o is for o rather
o is for onomatopoeia

p is for pigeon
gently gently
p is for panipuri
rashly rashly
p is for pearl chowdhry
brutally brutally
p is for piles ointment venkatraman brushed his teeth with

q is for q's for buses
q is for q's in ladies toilets
q is for quick said the bird

r is for rings on her fingers
r is for raj kapoor gaining in weight
r is for ricky ticky tick tick

s is for s. r. bhat
hopelessly hopelessly
s is for scorpio
venomously venomously
s is for the sense of direction
s is for the slip that shows

t is for trouble trouble
t is for tuffet who sat on a muffet
t is for the time we met first
t is just for the two of us

u is me
luckily luckily

v is for vaporub the princess ate
v is for vitamins
alphabetically

x is for things we dare not say
x is for things we dare not think
x is for things we dare not dream
x is for things we dare not do

y is for you go first
y is for YOU go first
y is for no you go first
y is for NO YOU go first

z is for himself alone
meanly
selfishly
self-centredly
egoistically
egocentrically
unscrupulously
caring for nobodyly

Three Cups of Tea

Song version

i didn't knock, the door said push, so i pushed my way
i didn't knock, the door said push, so i just pushed my way
i stood in front of the manager, i said i want my pay

he looked up and said you'll be paid on the first with all the rest
company rules he said you'll be paid on the first with all the rest
i merely picked up his watch it was on top of his desk

i said pick up the phone
call the cops i said just dial one o o
according to my rules baby i get paid when i say so

i said to my sister-in-law i want my share
sweetie pie i said to her i want my share
my brother can't have you all it's just not fair

rehman said you'll die for this and went for his gun
rehman said you'll die for this and went for his gun
kill me i said kill me for a bloody cunt

in burma i went for a film the man said where's your passport
the man at the window said i want to see your passport
hell with the ticket i said project the whole film up your asshole

they sent me back the cop said what took you to burma
they sent me back the pig grunted and said what took you to burma
prickface i said india is none of my karma

awards have many uses

awards have many uses
they silence the critics
convince the illiterates
confirm the faith of the few
who always believed in you
and underline the sponsor's commitment to excellence

and the money of course
always comes in handy
bringing unexpected relief
to struggling poets
just when the cash flow seemed to be drying up all around

awards are also like silver nails in the poet's coffin

they are a nice way of burying poets
who seemed to have been around for far too long
instead of dying early
as all good poets should

on the other hand
a poet is under no obligation
to stop writing
just because he is buried

i sincerely thank my undertakers
the bank of india and the panel of judges
but warn them
that my best is yet to come

i've laid by
enough supply of writing materials
in my burial chamber
to last me an eternity

i'm sure mr akbar padamsee here
and my other tombmates
have taken similar precautions

thank you
everybody

II From an Undated Sheet

I wrote all the poems that Dilip has translated[1] originally in Marathi. The majority of them were written between 1955-57. I also wrote English parallels for most of them at the same time but abandoned them as hopeless efforts.

I wrote 'Make Way Poet', 'Woman', 'Teeth', 'Suicide of Rama', 'Dreaming of Snakes', originally in English.

'Three Cups of Tea' is a translation of a poem I wrote not in Marathi but in some kind of street Hindi or 'Bambai' Hindi.

2 of my English versions have their Marathi equivalents. 'The Hag' I probably wrote first in English and 'Irani Restaurant Bombay' probably in Marathi. In fact, the writing in both cases could almost have been simultaneous.

'Irani Restaurant Bombay': While doing it in English I overtook the original Marathi version by adding one more stanza. The last stanza (in the English version) is absent in Marathi. To anyone reading it in both languages, it would appear as if the English version was the more complete one.

'Teeth' is an interesting case. In a way, I wrote it first in Marathi or started writing it, and although I have the rough drafts lying around somewhere to this day, in the hope of getting back to it, I never completed it. After completing the English poem, I took up the theme in Marathi again. More than once. But every time I found a new variation and came up with 3 different poems in Marathi.[2] I won't be surprised to find more Marathi poems coming out of it when I go back to it, as I keep promising myself.

Whenever I have written a version in both languages, I like to think of them as two original poems in two different languages rather than one a translation of the other.

1. *An Anthology of Marathi Poetry: 1945-65* (1967).
2. They are 'Anna', 'Chakki', and 'Chattamatta'. Kolatkar translated the last two as 'Song of the Flour Mill' and 'The Feast'; see section II, 'Poems in Marathi'.

III Making love to a poem

1

Translating a poem is like making love / having an affair

Making love to a poem / with the body of another language

You may meet a poem you like

Getting to know the poem carnally
   gaining carnal knowledge

A consenting poem
   having made sure that the poem is above the age of consent

Varieties of the experience
   if the poem is ready / game / willing
   it may need as much skill, patience, delicacy
   to consummate the act

Having got the poem into bed
you may discover you're not up to it
or that it's just not your day / or night

it follows that translating your own poems
   is like making love to one of your daughters
   it ought to be a cognisable offence
   taboo
   carry a stigma

there ought to be a law against translating your own poems
(unless the law against incest already covers it)
since it would be like seducing your own daughter

2

I can't translate a poem until I've got the feeling that I possess it
I must take possession of a poem before I can translate it

3

Tilak and Gandhi were bilingual writers

Some of the finest poetry in India, or indeed the world, has come
from a sense of alienation

It is the central experience of a lot of bhakti poetry for instance
    it's at the bottom of a lot of Dalit poetry
    it has given us poems like 'Cold Mountain'
    folk poetry   where women sing about their lot

4

'Only in one's mother-tongue can one express one's own truth. In
a foreign language, the poet lies.' – Paul Celan

'By submitting the German language to so intense a reduction that
he [Paul Celan] is, in effect, writing German like a foreign language.'
– Katherine Washburn and Margaret Guillemin, *Parnassus*, Spring/
Summer 1981.

'Celan took German poetry through a process of willed decompos-
ition.'

5

Ever since I began to write poems I have written in 2 languages (on
occasion in a 3rd language)
but I don't think I have written a bilingual poem in my life

A poem written in 2 languages
like Eknath did in the 16th century   Hindustani & Marathi
& Ram Joshi in the 19th century   Sanskrit & Marathi

I generally try not to let my left hand know what my right is doing

Bilingual poets may exist
a bilingual poem doesn't

I have a pen in my possession
which writes in 2 languages
and draws in one

My pencil is sharpened at both ends
I use one end to write in Marathi
the other in English

what I write with one end
comes out as English
what I write with the other
comes out as Marathi

6

Whether half my work will always remain invisible
like the other side of the moon
whether a reader in one language will have to be content
with the side facing him

Whether my work is 2 bodies of work   in spite of their common origin
which have developed independently of each other
each with its separate history
ecology   life forms
spin   rate of spin   temperature   tilt   tilt of axis
atmosphere
each moving in its own orbit

occasionally influencing each other   causing anomalies
in motion   or occasionally eclipsing one another
causing tidal waves   tides

A pencil sharpened at both ends   the bilingual poet waits
will he write his next poem in English
will he write it in Marathi

which language will he write the next poem in
will depend on which way his pencil points at the piece of paper
before him

what will he do if he wants to write a poem in Chinese
find a pencil which points three ways
buy a new pencil   brush

There is a neural selector switch in my brain
                    first I press the on button
                    when I see the light   pilot light
                    I press the selector switch

How do I write in 2 languages? On alternate days

Am I two different animals   or just one with a striped skin
                                          a piebald

           7
I've written in 2 languages from the start
I was writing what I hoped were poems
switching from the one to the other freely
without asking myself whether I had
the right to write in either

                              and riding rough shod over both
     or the qualifications
qualifications I knew I had none

I didn't have to ask myself what qualifications I had
for I knew the answer to that one   I had none

I went merrily along
writing one poem in Marathi after another in English
sometimes starting one in Marathi and finishing it in English
or vice versa
writing one in English and then rewriting it in Marathi
or the other way round
and abandoning many ideas

writing ten in one language   then a few in another
sometimes writing 3 altogether new poems
in an attempt to translate one
     or indulge in cannibalism

348

or sometimes constructing one poem
out of material taken from 10 discarded poems
stolen / salvaged / plundered
from rubbish heap / junkyard / graveyard

You need a double barreled gun to shoot a bilingual poet
one bullet in the head will never be enough to kill me
you need 2 bullets to kill me   for I'm two beasts
    you're hunting / tracking not one but 2 beasts
                though our tracks may crisscross
and we may come to the same waterhole to drink
        and to the same saltlicks
                there are two distinct scents we use
to mark the boundaries   we hunt in different parts of the jungle
                though our territories may overlap
or sometimes when our paths cross we may pass through each other
exchanging some of our characteristics in the process

    8
32 ways of skinning a bilingual poet

    9
Or whether it's only a reflection
of cultural schizophrenia
creative schizophrenia   split personality

Whether I'm just one poet writing in 2 languages
or in fact 2 poets writing in 2 different languages

whether I present one profile in one language
and another profile in the other

whether I'm a double agent
stealing the secrets of one language and selling them to the other
and vice versa

whether I practice a kind of psychological double bookkeeping

whether I'm truly ambidextrous
or whether I reserve / relegate one language for certain restricted /
                                                              unclean functions
which would be taboo in the other

whether I wipe my arse with one   eat with the other
                    use one to wipe my arse   one to eat with
or whether my use of 2 languages can be likened
to the way I use my 2 hands
relegating one to minor jobs or certain taboo functions

and leaving the other free to *[left incomplete]*
reserving one to do all the dirty work
and leaving the other free to do pretty well what it likes / wants to
                    a simple twist of mind
or whether the 2 sides of my creative personality
represented by work in 2 languages run into each other
to form a single continuous surface like a Möbius strip
    or whether my work taken in its entirety forms a Möbius strip
    the 2 sides running into each other and forming
    a single continuous surface

    10

Or whether I've done the sensible thing

I've bought plots in two cemeteries   graveyards
        booked space for myself
        dug my grave in 2 cemeteries
        I'll be buried in two coffins

        placed orders with 2 funeral parlours
            2 tombstones with epitaphs in 2 different languages

        why have I been digging my grave in 2 cemeteries
            a trick I learnt from Kabir
        when they look for my body they'll find flowers
                            before they come to blows
they'll only find some flowers   2 handfuls of flowers
which they will divide equally among   between them
and the 2 handfuls   they'll carry the 2 handfuls
to be buried in 2 separate graves

11

For an Indian robbed of his mother tongue
                    who has been robbed   disinherited
by his education   family background   cheated out of his
                                                    inheritance
there may be no alternative to writing in the only
language he knows   English
but why a person   someone like me who doesn't even have
that excuse should bother to write in it
may seem a mystery if not a crime   a cognisable offence
                    since there is at least as yet
                    no law against it
effectively preventing [him]
          from getting access   cultural inheritance
and cutting him off from much of daily life   the life   around him
shutting him out   depriving him

  a cultural bypass operation
opening wide windows   picture windows
in one wall   with sea view   westerly breeze
out of which   for him to look out of
boarding up another
so as to keep him from looking at what is happening in his own
                                                    backyard
a window to the world   wide world
cutting off his lifelines

12

'To create a poem means to translate from the mother tongue into another language... No language is the mother tongue. For that reason I do not understand when people speak of French or Russian poets. A poet can write in French, but he cannot be a French poet ... Orpheus exploded and broke up the nationalities, or stretched their boundaries so wide that they now include all nations, the dead and the living.'
– Marina Tsvetayeva in a letter to Rainer Maria Rilke

13

Every now and then someone comes along
to have a closer look at me   curiosity aroused
            to see if I'm real
and asks me whether I write in English as well as in Marathi
and this after I've made the admission myself

he or she   more often a young woman who describes herself
        as a journalist   or a postgraduate student
                on the lookout for a subject for her thesis
asks me
do you find it easier to write in Marathi or in English?

after making a few friendly noises   and stroking me gently on the head
        after   offering me a hand   raising an open hand
            to prove they're not armed they're clean
to which my answer of course has usually been that
I find writing in one language just as difficult
as writing in another

I find it equally difficult to write in either language
Easier? Well, I don't know

I don't expect writing to be easy for me in any language
if it was all that easy I'd probably have stopped writing long ago
I look at her pityingly   make a face   and say
the truth is that I've never found it easier to write in
one language than in the other
but when I say this for some reason they feel
                they're not getting a straight answer
or they feel I'm not being cooperative
                or sometimes they even take offence

14

Like it or not
I'll make you world famous
not you alone but both of us
we're going to be famous Tuka
you and I together

These translations are going to make me famous throughout the world

I'm going to teach you

You got to have some English Tuka
if you want to get ahead in the world

You don't care for fame, I know that

I'm not gonna pan off your poems as mine

Salo Malo tried that
    Sala Malo tried to pass off your poems as his
    that didn't work
    I'll try to pass off mine as yours

I'll create such confusion
that nobody can be sure about what you wrote and what I did

15

You are a lot of words
if I take them away
and replace them with others / substitute my own
what remains of Tuka
but the spaces between them

16

I say
I'm his legal heir
let 'em contest his will
Tuka has left me everything
everything he ever wrote
is mine by right
let 'em go to court
and argue their case for a hundred / thousand years
there are many who claim
to be his legal heirs

He himself was not above lifting whole verses
whole lines when it suited him

He won't miss a thing
and if he does he won't mind
and if he does what of it, he certainly won't complain
he dare not
I can trace the ownership of some of this stuff
to Namdeo

17

I may register / receive / read some of Mandelstam's poems in
                                                      translation
40 years after he died
or 60 years after he wrote them / went nova

It may take Mandelstam's light 40 years
to reach me
and then I may add his name to my star chart / map / catalogue
        and a dot may appear on my mental picture
        and a dot may appear where there was only
        darkness on the photographic plate of my consciousness

It may take 300 years for a Tukaram or a Villon or a Kabir
to be part of my consciousness
simply because I was born that much later
1300 years for Tu Fu to find a good translator a publisher
before he registers on my mind

18

Will the real Ramanujan please stand up
there are several of them as you know

A.K. Ramanujan is a legion rather than an individual

There is a multitude of Ramanujans
the poet of course, the translator, the folklorist

There are any number of A.K. Ramanujans
I am personally acquainted / familiar with at least 3 of them
and love 'em all

I don't claim to know all of them

I wonder whether the Real Ramanujan expresses himself
through his translations (rather than through his poems)

Ramanujan and his doubles

19

I'm aware of many of my contemporaries
only sketchily or as part of my peripheral vision
like a football player who while intent upon
dribbling the ball may have a map of the
entire field somewhere in his mind
    a precise map of the whole changing field
    at any given moment

I'm too busy with my own creative problems
               what I'm doing
                          writing at the moment
to really be able to see what's going on around me
              think too much about what the others
                      are occupied with

Although I'm aware of them peripherally as a football player
may be aware of the whole field as he himself
is intent upon dribbling the ball

I'll really have to see a replay of the whole
match after it's all over to be able to say
               anything about it or to learn
from it   trouble is I may either be dead
or carried off on a stretcher midway through the game

The map of the entire field is continually being
remade in the footballer's mind

20

'We great men are always modest.'
– Antonio Machado

AFTERWORD
What Is an Indian Poem?

Here are two poems. The language of the first, which I have transcribed in the Roman alphabet, is not English. However, it uses English words – 'manager', 'company', 'rule', 'table', 'police', 'complaint' – that readers will recognise. If one keeps only the English words and erases the rest, the poem will resemble a Sapphic fragment:

> main manager ko bola mujhe pagaar mangta hai
> manager bola company ke rule se pagaar ek tarikh ko milega
> uski ghadi table pay padi thi
> maine ghadi uthake liya
> aur manager ko police chowki ka rasta dikhaya
> bola agar complaint karna hai to karlo
> mere rule se pagaar ajhee hoga

The second poem is a translation of the first:

> i want my pay i said
> to the manager
> you'll get paid said
> the manager
> but not before the first
> don't you know the rules?
> coolly I picked up his
> wrist watch
> that lay on his table
> wanna bring in the cops
> i said
> 'cordin to my rules
> listen baby
> i get paid when i say so

The language (it is more of a patois) of the first poem is Bombay-Hindi; that of the translation is American English. Both poems are by Arun Kolatkar. He was a bilingual poet who wrote in Marathi and English. 'Main manager ko bola', which was written in 1960, is part of a sequence of three poems, all written in the same patois. The sequence, which does not have a title, first appeared in a Marathi little magazine and subsequently, in 1977, in Kolatkar's first collection of Marathi poems. In English, Kolatkar titled the sequence 'Three Cups of Tea'.

Occasionally, Kolatkar translated his Marathi poems into English, but he mostly kept the two separate. Sometimes he wondered what the connection between them was, or if there was any connection at all. Kolatkar created two very different bodies of work of equal distinction and importance in two languages. The achievement, I think, has few parallels in world literature. What has a parallel, at least in India, is that he drew, in his work, on a multiplicity of literary traditions. He drew on the Marathi of course, and Sanskrit, which he knew; he drew on the English and American traditions, especially Black American music and speech ('cordin to my rules / listen baby / I get paid when i say so'); and he drew on the European tradition. He drew on a few others besides. As he said in an interview once, talking about poets, 'Anything might swim into their ken.'

Fortunately, in Kolatkar's case, we know something about that 'anything'. Kolatkar died in September 2004. Recently, while going through his papers in Bombay, I came across a typed sheet in which Kolatkar had put down a chronology of his life. In it, against each year, he gave the name of the advertising agency he worked for at the time (Ajanta, National, Press Syndicate); the area of Bombay he lived in (Malad, Sion, A Road); illnesses, if any; and the poems he wrote, both English and Marathi. That is how we know when he wrote 'main manager ko bola'. He also gave the names of the authors he read that year. Against 1965, he mentions the following: 'Snyder, Williams, Villon, Lautréamont, Catullus, Belli, Apollinaire, Morgenstern, Berryman, Wang Wei, Tu Fu, Li Po, *Cold Mountain*'. *Cold Mountain* is the title of a book of translations of the Chinese poet known as Han Shan (Cold Mountain), whom, incidentally, Gary Snyder had also translated.

'Art', Ezra Pound said, 'does not exist in a vacuum.' And Claude Lévi-Strauss, 'Whether one knows it or not, one never walks alone along the path of "creativity".' Kolatkar's list of authors, which appears to be random, is in fact a capsule biography, a life of the life of the mind. Show me your books and I'll tell you who you are. It's a mind that could move with ease from 1st-century BC Italy to 8th-century China to 15th-century France to 20th-century America, while at the same time picking up the language spoken in the back-streets of Bombay, a slice of which he offers, without comment, in 'main manager ko bola'. But that said, the names of poets that appear in the list are not in themselves surprising. We were all reading the same or similar things in Bombay in 1965. There is, however, one exception to this, and that is Belli. Though his name belongs among the greatest in 19th-century European literature, he is known to very few, even in Italy. In the mid-60s, there was only one English translation of this poet around, and it's the one Kolatkar must have read. The translation is by Harold Norse and is called *The Roman Sonnets of G.G. Belli*. It has a preface by William Carlos Williams (a name that also figures in Kolatkar's list) and an introduction by Alberto Moravia. It was published by Jonathan Williams in 1960. What is striking about Harold Norse's translation is the idiom in which he translates Romanesco, the Roman dialect (perhaps not unlike Bombay-Hindi) in which Belli wrote his sonnets. Here is the opening sentence of Williams's preface:

> Gogol wanted to do the job, and D.H. Lawrence, each into his own language but they were written not into the classic language Italian that scholars were familiar with, but the Roman dialect that gave them an intimate tang which was their major charm and which the illustrious names spoken of above could not equal.

Coming to Norse's translation, Williams says:

> These translations are not made into English but into the American idiom in which they appear in the same relationship facing English as the original Roman dialect does to classic Italian.

'Three Cups of Tea' first appeared in Saleem Peeradina's anthology *Contemporary Indian Poetry in English* in 1972. The anthology was the first to represent the new Indian poetry in English, and 'Three Cups of Tea' has been a part of the canon since. I don't have a date for when Kolatkar made the translation, but I suspect it was made after 1965, after his discovery of Norse's Belli and the demotic American that Norse employs to translate Romanesco: 'If ya wanna be funny, it's enough to be / A gentleman.'

So there it is, your Indian poem. It was written in a Bombay patois by a poet who otherwise wrote in Marathi and English. It then became part of two literatures, Marathi and Indian English, but entered the latter in a translation made in the American idiom, one of whose sources, or, if you will, inspirations, was an American translation of a 19th-century Roman poet.

AKM

CHRONOLOGY

1931   1 November, Arun Balkrishna Kolatkar born in Kolhapur, the eldest child of Balkrishna Kolatkar (1901-79), an educationist, and Sitadevi (1910-95). Kolatkar himself, though, always gave 1932 as his year of birth. The discrepancy, according to family sources, arose because the wrong year was entered in the school record at the time of admission.

1937   Admitted to Modern High School, whose name is changed to Branch Rajaram High School in 1941.

1942   Encourages classmates to boycott school and participate in the Quit India movement.

1943   First sketches, which include portraits of Bhagat Singh.

1943-44 First poems and stories in *Jaltarang*, a handwritten magazine which he puts together with Baburao Sadwelkar and some other students.

1947   Matriculation from Bombay University; the subjects in which he is examined are Sanskrit, Marathi, physics and chemistry. Before the exams, reads the Katha and Kena Upanishads.

1948   Enrolls at Vadangekar Art School, Kolhapur; does sketches and landscapes and wins prize in art competition. Reads Bernard Shaw, P.G. Wodehouse, Jerome K. Jerome, James Jeans and Richard Aldington.

1949   Admitted to J.J. School of Art, Bombay; befriends Ambadas, who is a student there. Reads *Lust for Life*, Yeats's *Oxford Book of Modern Verse*, Dostoevsky, Bergson and C.E.M. Joad. Father posted to Pune as assistant education inspector.

1950   Continues at the J. J. School of Art.

1951   Leaves the J.J. School of Art midway through the course; befriends Bandu Waze. Reads Dnyaneshwar's *Amrutanubhav*, Tukaram, Bahirat, Manmohun, Kusumagraj and Mardhekar.

1952   Lives in Pune. For a while, considers working in a school as art teacher and does a special "advanced" course to qualify for the job; paints abstracts. Befriends Ashok Kelkar. Reads Whitman, T.S. Eliot, Rilke, Dylan Thomas, Edith Sitwell, Christopher Fry, Jacques Maritain, Ouspensky's *Tertium Organum*, J. Krishnamurti, Sri Aurobindo and *Partisan Review*.

1953   April-May, goes on a walking trip through western Maharashtra with Bandu Waze; writes the 'journey poems'. Spends the rest of the year mostly at Pune, but does not live with the family; also spends time at Gudgeri, near Hubli in Karnataka, where he has cousins, and at Kolhapur. Ambadas introduces him to Darshan Chhabda. Reads Sri Ramakrishna, Lin Yutang, D.H. Lawrence, Neruda and Frost.

1954   18 March, marries Darshan Chhabda. Visit to Bhor and Nasik, where he writes 'In a godforsaken hotel'. Lives in various lodges in Colaba, Girgaum and Malad, before finally renting a room in Malad. Either this year or the next, in response to an advertisement in the *Times of India*, applies for a job as office peon. Befriends Dilip Chitre and Ashok Shahane. Reads the Elizabethans, Donne, Hopkins, Yeats, Pound, Auden, Emily Dickinson, E.E. Cummings and Demetrios Kapetanakis.

1955   Through M.F. Husain, gets a job in a Malad toyshop to paint wooden toys. Publishes his first Marathi poem in *Satyakatha* and his first English poem, 'The Renunciation of the Dog', in *Quest*; meets Nissim Ezekiel. Befriends Ramesh Samartha and becomes part of a group that publishes *Shabda*, a cyclostyled Marathi poetry magazine. Leaves Bombay for Madras.

1956   Spends the year in Madras. In April, applies for the job of assistant artist at Ground Training School, Air Force Station, Tambaram, but nothing comes of it; learns Morse, in the expectation of finding employment as a telegraph operator. To earn money, paints clay pots and tries to market them. Meets some of the Madras poets and writers, Sri Sri, Arudra, Gora Sastri and Bairagi. Reads Kierkegaard, Baudelaire, Rimbaud, Wallace Stevens, Theodore Roethke, Hart Crane, Kafka, Beckett, Donald Davie and Oscar Williams's *Pocket Book of Modern Verse*. Father appointed deputy director of education, Maharashtra.

1957   Returns to Bombay and completes his diploma at J.J. School of Art, standing first in order of merit. In June, joins Ajanta Advertising as visualiser. Reads Ionesco, Pound's *Cantos* and Heller's *Catch-22*. Father retires and is given a year's extension.

1959   October, quits Ajanta to join National Advertising, the first Indian-owned ad firm, as senior visualiser; befriends Kersy Katrak, who is employed at the same agency. Meets Dom Moraes, who describes him and Dilip Chitre as 'two young Maharashtrian novelists who look exactly like Rimbaud and Verlaine' (*Gone Away*, 1960).

1961   January, quits National Advertising to join Bomas; transferred to Kolkata as art director at the end of the year.

1962   April, diagnosed with 'peptic ulcer with pyloric stenosis'; returns to Bombay. Befriends Allen Ginsberg and Peter Orlovsky. Does the Tukaram translations. Loses job at the end of the year. Reads 'The Seafarer'.

1963   Unemployed for six months, during which he writes 'the boatride'. Joins Press Syndicate.

1964   December, visits Jejuri with his brother Makarand and Manohar Oak, and writes poems based on the visit.

1965   March, operated for stomach ulcer at Dr Bacha's Nursing Home; April-June, writes the 'Hospital Poems'. Reads Williams Carlos Williams, Berryman, Snyder, Villon, Lautréamont, Apollinaire, Catullus, G.G. Belli, Christian Morgenstern, Wang Wei, Li Po, Tu Fu and *Cold Mountain*.

1966   January, resigns from Press Syndicate to start Design Unit with four other partners. One of the Jejuri poems, 'A Low Temple', is published in *Dionysus*, but the magazine's editors lose the rest of the manuscript and it is never found again. Befriends Gieve Patel. Period of heavy drinking, which extends into the next two years.

1967   Befriends Adil Jussawalla and Arvind Krishna Mehrotra. His campaign for Liberty shirts wins Air India Trophy for campaign of the year. November-December, Design Unit closes down.

1968   July-August, joins Kersy Katrak's Mass Communication and Marketing (MCM), the agency which is supposed to have revolutionised Indian advertising. 'the boatride' published in *damn you*, no. 6. Befriends Kiran Nagarkar.

1969   Becomes keenly interested in pop music, the Beatles, Bob Dylan, blues, what he calls 'rock in general'; begins to write song lyrics, some of them recalling incidents from his drinking days; goes teetotal. April, divorce from Darshan Chhabda. Does the drawings for *The Policeman: A wordless play in thirteen scenes*. Kiran Nagarkar joins MCM as copywriter; December, MCM moves offices from Oliver Street to Bakhtavar, opposite the Colaba Post Office.

1970   5 May, marries Soonoo Katrak. August, moves into a paying guest accommodation in Bakhtavar, on the same floor as MCM. Befriends Arjun Shejwal, from whom he learns the pakhawaj; also, separately, takes guitar lessons. His campaign for Hindustan Machine Tools wins Air India Trophy for campaign of the year.

1973   Aiming to break into the international pop scene, records a demo with four songs. November-December, begins work on *Jejuri*.

1974   March, completes *Jejuri*, whose first reader is Kersy Katrak; *Jejuri* published in *Opinion Literary Quarterly* (monsoon issue). Befriends *Balwantbua*. Reads Mandelstam, Akhmatova, Tsvetayeva, Vallejo, Rózewicz, Tranströmer, Amichai, Ted Hughes, Mark Strand and Charles Simic.

1975   MCM taken into liquidation. Again jobless, he teams up with Kiran Nagarkar and for the next six years they freelance; most of the work they get is from Pratibha.

1976   *Jejuri* published by Clearing House; begins writing the poems collected in *Chirimiri*.

1977   February, *Arun Kolatkarchya Kavita* published by Pras; September, *Jejuri* wins the Commonwealth Poetry Prize; *Arun Kolatkarchya Kavita* wins the H.S. Gokhale Award; the Marathi little magazine *Rucha* brings out special Kolatkar number.

1978   January, *Kavi India* brings out special Kolatkar number. May, first visit abroad, to England, to give a reading from *Jejuri* at the Commonwealth Institute. German translation by Günther D. Sontheimer of his Marathi 'Black Poems' published as Heidelberger Südasien-Texte 4.

1979   Participates in Struga Poetry Evenings, Yugoslavia.

1981   September, leaves Bakhtavar and moves into his own apartment in Prabhadevi.

1982   Joins Chaitra as creative director, but works only part-time to devote himself to *Balwantbua*. Visits England, to read at the Festival of India.

1984   German translation by Giovanni Bandini of *Jejuri* published by Verlag Wolf Mersch. Quits Chaitra.

1985   Joins Kersy Katrak's new ad agency, Fulcrum. Completes the first draft of Balwantbua. Visits France, reads at the Pompidou Centre as part of the Festival of India.

1986   May, visits the United States, as part of the Festival of India, and gives readings in various cities, including one at the Museum of Modern Art, New York; meets Allen Ginsberg. October, participates in the Frankfurt Book Fair.

1987   Visits Sweden, to read at the Festival of India. Joins Lintas, where

Kersy Katrak has moved after closing down Fulcrum; thereafter, Kolatkar shifts to the Lintas subsidiary SSC&B.

1989   January, participates in the World Poetry Festival, Bhopal. The audience finds the language of one of the poems he reads there to be obscene, which amuses the world poets, who, later, speak in his defence. Nominated to the Communication Artists Guild hall of fame for lifetime achievement.

1991   Balwantbua dies.

1992   Arjun Shejwal dies.

1994   Conferred the Kusumagraj Award.

1995   Conferred the Bahinabai Chaudhuri Kavya Puraskar.

1999   Conferred the Bank of India Excellence Award for literature.

2000   Baburao Sadwelkar dies.

2002   January, Wayside Inn, his hangout for almost thirty years and the venue of his Thursday afternoons, shuts down.

2003   His contract with SSC&B is not renewed and he is forced into retirement. February, *Chirimiri* published; November, *Bhijki Vahi* published.

2004   30 March, diagnosed with stomach cancer; 5 May, receives the Keshavrao Kothavale Paritoshik for *Bhijki Vahi* in Pune; 11 July, screening of Dilip Chitre's Sahitya Akademi film on Kolatkar at Prithvi Theatre, Juhu; 14 July, *Kala Ghoda Poems*, *Sarpa Satra*, and *Droan*, a long poem in Marathi, published; 17 July, reads his Marathi poems at Lok Vangmaya Griha, Prabhadevi; 22-23 September, has his last conversations with friends who have gathered in Pune; 25 September, dies.

NOTES

The notes to *Jejuri*, *Kala Ghoda Poems* and *Sarpa Satra* were made by Laetitia Zecchini, Centre National de la Recherche Scientifique (CNRS), Paris. All other notes are by Arvind Krishna Mehrotra.

JEJURI (42-72)

Jejuri, a pilgrim town in the western Indian state of Maharashtra, is best known for its temple to Khandoba, a folk deity whose other names are Martanda, Mhalsakant (husband of Mhalsa), Mallari, and Mallanna. Khandoba is also worshipped as a form of Shiva who descended to become king on Earth and hold court in the hill fort of Jejuri. The cult of Khandoba is characteristic of a syncretic memory in which Sanskrit and brahmanical traditions, folk religion and themes, popular practices, legends and rituals constantly interact; also see note to 'The Horseshoe Shrine' below.

For more on Jejuri and the Khandoba cult see *Flags of Fame, Studies in South Asian Folk Culture*, eds. Heidrun Bruckner, Lothar Lutze, Aditya Malik (Delhi: Manohar, 1993) and two of Gunther-Dietz Sontheimer's books: *King of Hunters, Warriors and Shepherds: Essays on Khandhoba*, eds. Anne Feldhaus, Aditya Malik, Heidrun Bruckner (Delhi: Manohar, 1997) and *Pastoral Deities in Western India* (Delhi: OUP, 1993). Kolatkar himself knew Sontheimer well and was familiar with his work: 'Have a look, sometime at the book by Gunther Sontheimer, *Pastoral Deities in Western India*. He's trying to preserve the oral traditions of this area. He feels too much emphasis has been placed on texts and not enough on the oral traditions of people actually practising religion' (Arun Kolatkar, *Talking Poems, Conversations with Poets*, ed. Eunice de Souza [Delhi: OUP, 1999], p. 18).

The Priest (43)
2.3 *puran poli*: 'Stuffed bread', a popular sweet in Maharashtra and other parts of South India. It is often given as offering to the deity.

Heart of Ruin (44)
1.1 *Maruti*: Another name for the monkey-god Hanuman, Lord Rama's ardent devotee and faithful companion in the *Ramayana*.

Chaitanya (47, 50, 66)
Title: Bengali reformer, preacher, and 'saint' who lived between 1486 and 1534. He is one of the *bhakti* poets who, between the 15th and 17th centuries, formed a powerful non-exclusive movement of popular devotion that opposed the brahmanical order while producing extraordinary poetry in the vernaculars; for Kolatkar's translations of Marathi *bhakti* poets, with whose work he was deeply familiar, see *The Boatride and Other Poems*, IV Translations. Chaitanya is said to have visited Jejuri and later settled in Orissa. Chaitanya preached a passionate and exclusive devotion to Krishna ('Krishna bhakti'). He rejected the social and religious orthodoxies, the complex intricacies of rituals and

temple worship to advocate the purification of faith through the loving absorption in a personal God and the chanting of God's name (notably popularising the Hare Krishna mantra). In the Bengali tradition, he is represented as an ecstatic and wandering mystic.

2.6 *Zendu*: Marigold, a flower commonly offered to Hindu gods.

A Low Temple (47)
15 *charminar*: Popular Indian brand of filterless cigarette.
16 *twenty foot tortoise*: Stone tortoise coated with brass outside the Khandoba temple. It is also where *kirtans* (devotional hymns) and dance performances in honor of the god are held. See next poem 'The Pattern'.

The Horseshoe Shrine (48)
2.2 *Khandoba*: Presiding deity of Jejuri, king of hunters, warriors and shepherds, demon-slayer, protector of sheep and cattle. He is considered to be particularly responsive to vows and is worshipped by people from all castes; some of his devotees are Muslims. He has five wives and his second marriage is a love-match with a shepherdess called Banai. Khandoba carried her off on his horse during one of his numerous hunting and amorous expeditions. In traditional iconography he is depicted on horseback with one or two of his wives. There's a place in Jejuri which is actually worshipped as 'ghode uddan', where the hoof of Khandoba's horse is imprinted on a stone.

Manohar (49)
Title: Manohar Oak (1933-93), Marathi poet and novelist, active in the 'little magazine' movement in Marathi in the 1960s. He accompanied Kolatkar on the trip to Jejuri in 1964.

Hills / The Priest's Son (51/52)
The hills around Jejuri are associated with Khandoba legends that often revolve around his victory over demons.

Ajamil and the Tigers (54)
An oral folk legend associated with the Khandoba cult. 'The story was that the vaghyas [tiger people] couldn't get enough to eat because of a zealous sheepdog. So they had to agree to conditions laid down by Ajamil. He'd give them a sheep and they had to bark like dogs. So they lost their 'tigeritude'! They had to become non-violent. Writing that poem was a way to understand that story. This is the only vaghya origin story I've heard' (Arun Kolatkar, *Talking Poems, Conversations with Poets*, p. 18).

A Song for a Vaghya (56)
Vaghyas are the male disciples of the deity and also his bards. Though their origin myth associates them with tigers, they have traditionally taken pride in being associated with dogs, which in popular devotion represents the self-humiliation of the devotee before God. On special occasions, vaghyas even behave like dogs, barking and eating from a begging bowl. They often carry a tiger-skin pouch with turmeric powder inside. This poem, like 'Ajamil and the Tigers', draws on the many different meanings and associations of the

protean vaghya identity (tiger, dog, devotee, bard, etc).

2.6 *turmeric*: An essential element of the Khandoba cult. It is the poor man's substitute for gold and represents the substance of God. During important Jejuri festivals, everything is immersed in it.

6.2 *this instrument / has one string*: The instrument is the ektara (alternately called *iktar* or *ektar*), traditionally used in devotional singing and popular all over India, especially with sadhus, wandering bards, and ascetics; it is also mentioned in 'The Blue Horse'.

A Song for a Murli (58)

Murlis are Khandoba's female devotees, courtesans, and wives. Before the practice was banned, murlis dedicated to Khandoba were often forced into 'sacred' prostitution. Both vaghyas and murlis sing, dance, and perform the deeds of Khandoba, especially during night-long vigils in return for the fulfillment of a vow.

1.2 *the moon has come down to graze / along the hill top*: According to Sontheimer, Khandoba is also a combination of the sun god Surya (see the last poem in the book, 'The setting sun') and Shiva, who is associated with the moon.

The Reservoir (58)

Peshwas: From 1749 to 1818, the Peshwas were the rulers of the Maratha Empire, which corresponded to most of central India, including what is today known as the state of Maharashtra.

A Little Pile of Stones (59)

At Jejuri, new brides offer little piles of stones to Khandoba. If the pile does not collapse, the bride is assured of marital bliss.

Makarand (60)

Title: Kolatkar's younger brother, who accompanied him and Manohar Oak to Jejuri in 1964.

2.2 *pooja*: personal act of worship or prayer ceremony.

The Temple Rat (61)

6.4 *linga*: An oval, phallic stone traditionally associated with the devotion of Shiva and often worshipped by oblations of milk and water. See 'Yeshwant Rao': 'mass of basalt, / bright as any post box, / the shape of protoplasm / or a king size lava pie / thrown against the wall, / without an arm, a leg / or even a single head.' These aniconic representations of god alternate with the anthropomorphic iconography of Khandoba on horseback.

A Kind of a Cross (62)

Title: The 'cross' refers to the instrument used in one of the mortification rites (here, the swinging of devotees suspended from hooks) associated with Khandoba worship.

Yeshwant Rao (64)

Title: According to legend, Yeshwant Rao was a member of the untouchable caste who sacrificed his life for Khandoba and was able to persuade the deity to stay on earth. He is the gatekeeper of Khandoba's temple and has a shrine near the main entrance of the fort. As a perfect embodiment of ardent devotion and self-sacrifice, Yeshwant Rao is today worshipped as a god and is famous for healing bone fractures.

6.11 *as he himself has no heads, hands and feet*: See note to 'The Temple Rat' above. Kolatkar plays on the nirguna (without attributes or qualities) aspect of god by writing about him in a most matter-of-fact way.

KALA GHODA POEMS (74-182)

Pi-dog (75)

1.7.1 *the equestrian statue of what's his name*: This refers to the black stone statue of King Edward VII mounted on a horse from which the Kala Ghoda (i.e. black or dark horse) neighbourhood of South Bombay takes its name; also see 'David Sassoon', section 9. In 1956, the statue was removed to another part of town. The space once occupied by it forms a traffic island that 'doubles as a parking lot' where, in the mornings, the street life of Kala Ghoda converges; see 'Breakfast Time at Kala Ghoda'.

2.3.1 *Old Woman's Island...Mahim*: Bombay originally consisted of seven disjointed islands (Isle of Bombay, Colaba, Old Woman's Island, Mahim, Mazagaon, Parel, Worli) that were gradually reclaimed from the sea.

4.1.3 *Yudhisthira / on his last journey*: Yudhisthira, Sahadeva, Nakul, Arjuna and Bhima are the five Pandava brothers in the *Mahabharata*. The last journey refers to The Great Departure episode, at the very end of the epic, in which the Pandavas and their wife Draupadi decide to renounce the world. They die one after the other, and their death is attributed to a violation of dharma (the order which regulates the universe and defines the behaviour of each caste). At the very end of the journey, God calls the last brother, Yuthisthira, to heaven and asks him to leave his dog behind. Since Yuthisthira, true to his dharma, refused to part with the faithful animal, he was saved and indeed 'airlifted' to heaven.

6.8.2 *in the Gayatri metre*: the mantra here referred to is the Gayatri mantra, also called Savitri mantra. It is the most revered mantra of the *Rg Veda* and of the Hindu tradition. This twenty-four syllable hymn in Sanskrit is a meditation on 'the divine Light' and was initially meant to be recited only by Brahmin males. The last two lines of the section, 'May the sun-god amplify / the powers of my mind', are a literal translation of the Sanskrit words in stanza 9. That a vagrant, mixed-breed pi-dog should recite these sacred words is of course an extreme case of inappropriateness.

Parameshwari (82)

Title: Another name of Durga, Shiva's consort, fearless goddess, and demon-slayer.

5.1 *the Kutchi witch*: From Kutch, a district in the western Indian state of Gujarat. Here as elsewhere in *Kala Ghoda Poems*, Kolatkar celebrates the communal mix and composite history of Bombay, a city of immigrants that has been like a magnet for people from every part of the Indian subcontinent.

Meera (86)

3.7.3 *gulmohur*: A deciduous tree with fern-like leaves and large flamboyant red and yellow flowers; also mentioned in 'The Barefoot Queen of the Crossroads' and 'Words for a Cellist'.

6.3.1 *like a Meera before her Lord*: Meera Bai, Mira or Mirabai (*c.* 1498-1546/ 1565), is a woman *bhakti* poet (see 'Chaitanya' in the notes to Jejuri). She is one of the most cherished and popular female figures in India whose poems are sung throughout the subcontinent. The countless legends on her life draw from a biography as flexible as the oral traditions which transmitted her poetry. The poetry *of* Meerabai and *on* Meerabai are inseparable. She was a Rajput princess married at a very early age to the Prince of Mewar but who maintained throughout her life that her real husband and only love was Krishna – for whom she used to dance and sing ecstatically. Her compositions celebrate her ardent relationship with the deity. They express the folly and the violence of love, the pain of desire and the beauty of the beloved, the pangs of separation and of desertion. Hers are songs of praise and rapture, of supplication and distress, but of rebellion as well. Meera overturned the normative values of Hinduism and the conventions of a patriarchal society to celebrate an uninhibited devotion to her god-lover (Krishna) rather than fidelity to her legitimate husband.

Song of Rubbish (89)

5.2 *tryst with destiny*: A reference to the opening words of a speech by Jawaharlal Nehru on the eve of India's independence on 15 August 1947: 'Long years ago we made a tryst with destiny...'

An Old Bicycle Tyre (104)

1.2.2 *shunya*: 'Void' or 'emptiness', it also stands for the numeral zero.

To a Charas Pill (117)

Title: Charas is 'lowgrade hash' (see the previous poem 'Knucklebones'). It is sold in the form of a pill, which is then broken, mixed with tobacco, and smoked in a *chillum*.

11.1 *Hindu Kush*: a 500-mile mountain range stretching between Pakistan and Afghanistan.

A Game of Tigers and Sheep (118)

The Pras Prakashan edition of *Kala Ghoda Poems* has, on the cover designed by Kolatkar, a photograph of a checkerboard drawn in charcoal on a paving stone, with yellow flowers fallen on it, interrupting the game.

3.1 *rusty shield-bearer*: Another name for the copper-pod; also called yellow flame tree or yellow flamboyant.

The Barefoot Queen of the Crossroads (120)

1.9.2 *choli*: Short blouse worn with a sari.

4.1.2 *Queen's Step-well*: Rani-ki-Vav, an 11th century step-well in the western state of Gujarat, in which water can be reached by going down several steps. It is one of the largest and most richly-sculptured of its type.

4.6.1 *Peeping Tom*: See note to 'David Sassoon' below.

Breakfast Time at Kala Ghoda (125)

4.4.3 *Gola*: Name of a nomadic tribe from the Telugu-speaking southern state of Andhra Pradesh.

5.2.2 *dalit*: The literal meaning of 'dalit' is 'oppressed' or 'crushed'. It is a name dalits have chosen themselves, in reaction to, and in protest against, the journalistic, bureaucratic or Hinduised names they were earlier called by, 'Untouchables', Scheduled Castes, and 'Harijan', the last, which means Children of God, given by Mahatma Gandhi. Dalit is now collectively applied to communities who are outside the Hindu caste system and have for centuries been discriminated against by the upper castes.

5.4.2 *jowar*: Sorghum.

6.2.2 *kanji*: Beverage made by fermenting carrot or beetroot juice.

6.8.3 *Ma Chudaos*: A common term of abuse; it translates as 'mother-fucker'.

9.5.1 *Serendip*: A former name of Sri Lanka.

9.5.3 *subcontinental in proportion*: The two traffic islands, 'the lesser island' and 'the much larger one', are like Sri Lanka and India, as seen in a map.

13.2.1 *divide-and-rule*: British imperial policy in India is often characterised as 'divide and rule', the 'divide' referring to creating divisions within Indian society, particularly along religious and sectarian lines.

16.4.2 *Gauri*: Another name of Shiva's demon-slaying consort Durga; by giving idlis to the 'homeless', Durga/Gauri slays 'the demon of hunger'.

Words for a Cellist (145)

3.3 *Max Muller Bhavan*: The German cultural centre in Kala Ghoda.

The Shit Sermon (146)

3.6.1-3 *Usne sabko diyela hai / - khaneko muh, / hugneko gaand*: The words, spoken in Bombay Hindi, are translated in the previous stanzas, 'He has given all his creatures [...]// two holes: / a feedhole and a shithole'.

5.3.1 *given in dowry*: The archipelago of what is today known as Bombay was part of the Portuguese princess Catherine de Braganza's dowry when she married King Charles II in 1661.

The Rat-poison Man's Lunch Hour (162)

1.2.1 *Wayside Inn*: Kala Ghoda restaurant and Kolatkar's favourite hangout (he is pictured there in the front cover photograph of *Collected Poems in English*); see Introduction and, for description, section 4 of poem; the restaurant is also mentioned in 'Lice' and 'Breakfast Time at Kala Ghoda, sections 7 and 9. The window table that Kolatkar usually occupied, with an unobstructed view of the traffic islands, gave him an extraordinary vantage point from which to observe the street-life of Kala Ghoda.

4.7.1 *Babasaheb*: Affectionate and respectful term dalits use (see 'Breakfast Time at Kala Ghoda', section 5) when referring to Bhimrao Ramji Ambedkar (1891-1956), one of India's great political leaders and chief architect of the Indian constitution. A dalit himself, he was also the first of his community to study in Great Britain. His dream of a 'society undivided by caste and creed' remains largely unfulfilled.

4.9.1 *obscure poet*: Bal Sitaram Mardhekar (1909-56), a far from obscure modernist Marathi poet, the title of whose best known poem 'Pipat mele olyo undir'

(Mice died in the wet barrel) is referred to in the next line.

5.1.2 *Aasamaa pe hai khuda*: 'There's God in heaven'; song from the 1958 Bollywood film *Phir subah hogi* starring Raj Kapoor and Mala Sinha.

6.9.1 *thali*: An Indian meal comprising a selection of different dishes, served on a metal platter or flat dish.

David Sassoon (169)

David Sassoon (1792-1864) fled Baghdad for Persia and then settled in India to become one of the most influent merchants of his time and the leader of the Jewish community in Bombay. His grave is in Pune but his 'pilloried' head in stone indeed sticks out of a medallion above the David Sassoon library archway in Kala Ghoda. The plaque below it reads: 'In 1847, a group of young mechanics and foremen of the Royal Mint and Government Dockyard decided to establish a museum and library of mechanical models and architectural designs, which led to the creation of the Sassoon Library. The oldest library in the city, it is a Venetian Neo-Gothic structure, designed by Gostling and Campbell and completed in 1870. The building houses a statute of Sir David Sassoon, a Sephardic Jew who donated Rs. 60,000 in 1863 for its construction. The Sassoon family also funded the equestrian statue of King Edward VII which gave the area its name – Kala Ghoda. An extensive conservation programme was launched for the building in 1996.'

David Sassoon appears also in 'The Barefoot Queen of the Crossroads', section 4 ('And if that peeping Tom / with the rabbinical beard / and a Persian potentate's turban, / / sticking his head out of a hole / above the library archway') and in 'The Shit Sermon', section 4 ('the fossilised upstart from Baghdad / / with his talmudic beard, / looking down on him / from above the library arch').

1.3.2 *ahmaq*: Persian-Urdu word for fool.

1.3.3 *keer-e-khar*: Persian for donkey's dick.

3.3.3 *five thousand seven hundred and forty-six*: The year the poem was written, 1985-86 in the Gregorian calendar.

9.7.1-2 *Hornby Road – or whatever they call it now*: Like the city of Bombay that was renamed Mumbai by the far-right Hindu nationalists (the Shiv Sena) in 1995, the names of roads and institutions too have been 'nationalised' or 'indigenised'. Hornby Road has become Dadabhai Naoroji Road, the Prince of Wales Museum is Chhatrapati Shivaji Maharaj Vastu Sangrahalaya, etc.

Man of the Year (178)

Title: A local custom in which a stuffed effigy (the man of the year) is set alight on the night of December 31.

SARPA SATRA (184-214)

Referring to his early poems like 'The Hag' and 'Irani Restaurant Bombay', Kolatkar has said that 'Whenever I have written a version in both languages [English and Marathi], I like to think of them as two original poems in two different languages rather than one a translation of the other' (*The Boatride and Other Poems*, Appendix II, 'From an Undated Sheet'). The English and

Marathi versions of *Sarpa Satra* (Snake Sacrifice) were written more or less simultaneously. The latter appeared in *Bhijki Vahi* (2003), literally 'sodden notebook', a reference to the drowned manuscript of the 17th-century Marathi *bhakti* poet Tukaram. The title, and particularly the cover, designed by Kolatkar and having, against a black background, the hieroglyph for tear (a crying eye), also refer to the theme of the book, for *Bhijki Vahi* revolves around the archetypal motif of the weeping woman; see Introduction.

Sarpa Satra proposes a re-reading of the opening myth of the *Mahabharata* which, like a lot of epics, is embedded in a frame narrative. The epic narrates the struggle, between two branches of the same family: the Kauravas and the Pandavas. This opening myth is one of the many apocalyptic rites of the *Mahabharata*, a *mise en abyme* of the cosmic antagonism which is the central drama of the epic, and which mirrors the numerous fratricidal conflicts of a narrative full of echoes and ramifications: conflicts between gods and demons, Kauravas and Pandavas, Kshatriyas and Brahmins, but also in the battlefield of the heart itself between *dharma* as the divine law and order and *adharma*, referring to chaos, injustice and disorder. *Sarpa Satra* is also a contemporary tale, the mass killings in the poem echoing twentieth-century genocides, holocausts and tales of revenge, and not only of the 20th century.

Janamejaya (186)
Janamejaya is a descendant of the protagonists of the *Mahabharata*. He performs the sacrifice to obtain the extermination of snakes – one of whom, Takshaka, the 'scheming snake' mentioned in the first line of *Sarpa Satra*, had killed his father, Parikshit, grandson of Arjuna and sole survivor of the Pandavas.
1.16.2 *slippery sons of Kadru*: Kadru is the ancestral mother of snakes. She cursed her offspring and promised they would die by fire, hence foreshadowing the snake sacrifice.

Jaratkaru speaks to her son Aastika (188)
Jaratkaru is a snake woman and victim of the sacrifice. Aastika, which literally means 'devout', is her son from an ascetic.
1.23.1 *yajnya*: sacrifice, the central notion and rite of Vedic religion.
1.25.1 *thread ceremony*: The Hindu ceremony called 'upanayana', a rite-of-passage ritual reserved for young high-caste boys, which initiates them into the knowledge of the Vedas, rituals, and sacrifices.
1.45.3 *the great Vyasa*: The alleged original author of the *Mahabharata* and an important character in the epic.
2.1.2 *Takshaka*: The 'scheming snake' Janamejaya mentions in the first line of *Sarpa Satra*; he is also Jaratkaru's brother.
2.8.3 *the Khandava forest*: The burning down of the Khandava forest is an essential episode of the *Mahabharata*. It was reduced to ashes by two of the most revered protagonists of the epic, Arjuna, the third Pandava brother, and Krishna. Takshaka's wife died in the conflagration and he in return killed Arjuna's grandson, Parikshit – thus sparking off an endless cycle of revenge. For the Sanskrit scholar and Indologist Madeleine Biardeau, the Khandava forest is a kind of 'miniature cosmos'.
2.20.2 *a crosscousin of his, / a cronie*: Krishna.
2.23.3 *gada*: A mace; a club.

2.54.2 *Partha*: Another name for Arjuna.

3.5.1 *Vaishampayana*: a Brahmin disciple of Vyasa, from whose lips he first heard the story and who then recites it to Janamejaya during the snake sacrifice.

3.36.3 *black dhotis, black shawls / and black pigskin slippers to match*: In the great snake sacrifice, as narrated in the *Mahabharata*, the officiating priests were indeed clad in black and wore black pigskin slippers.

3.44.3 *Shesha*: One of the primal beings of Creation, the many-headed king of snakes (the Nagas), closely associated with Vishnu. In post-Vedic mythology, the universe is sustained and supported by Shesha. Shesha also means 'what is left'; this residue, surviving destruction after each cosmic dissolution, guarantees the recreation of the world.

3.46.1 *rakhi*: A talisman that sisters tie on the arm of their brothers on the day of the Raksha Bandhan ('bond of protection') festival.

3.51.1 *Khatam*: Finished.

3.78.2 *holocaust*: Here used in its primary meaning of 'sacrifice', particularly sacrifice by fire.

3.85.3 *squirming Om sign*: Om is used as a mantra or auspicious formula at the beginning of prayers; its symbol resembles the coiled silhouettes of snakes clinging to each other.

3.114.1 *Vasuki Mama*: Mama means maternal uncle; Vasuki is Jaratkaru's brother and thus Aastika's uncle.

The Ritual Bath (212)

20.3 *rakshasas*: Malignant demons.

THE BOATRIDE AND OTHER POEMS (216-355)

ABBREVIATIONS

AAMP   *An Anthology of Marathi Poetry: 1945-65*, edited by Dilip Chitre (Bombay: Nirmala Sadanand Publishers, 1967)

AKK   *Arun Kolatkarchya Kavita* (Bombay: Pras Prakashan: 1977)

KP   Kolatkar Papers

PERI   *Periplus*, edited by Daniel Weissbort and Arvind Krishna Mehrotra (Delhi: Oxford University Press, 1993)

TMIP   *Oxford India Anthology of Twelve Modern Indian Poets*, edited by Arvind Krishna Mehrotra (Delhi: Oxford University Press, 1992)

TBAG   *Tukaram bavanchya abhanganchi gatha* (Bombay: Government of Bombay, 1869-1873; rpt. 1950)

I *Poems in English 1953-1967* (218-30)

The Renunciation of the Dog (218)

Written 1953. One of the 'journey poems'; see Introduction. This was Kolatkar's first published poem in English and appeared in the inaugural issue of *Quest* (August 1955). Reprinted in *Ten Years of Quest* (1966), edited by Abu Sayeed Ayyub and Amlan Datta. There is a companion poem to it in AKK, which Kolatkar translated as 'The Turnaround'; see 'Poems from the Marathi'.

3 *Barking at the waves*: The sea at the Gateway of India, Bombay, where Kolatkar and his friend, the poet and painter Bandu Vaze, spent the night before setting out on the walking trip; see Introduction.

10-12 The incident of the dog also figures in 'The Turnaround'; see Introduction.

Of an origin moot as cancer's (218)

Written 1953. Text from KP. One of the 'journey poems'; see Introduction. Also written in Marathi, this was Kolatkar's first published poem in Marathi and appeared in the Diwali 1954 issue of *Satyakatha*. Marathi title 'Ghoda'; collected in AKK.

Dual (219)

Written 1954/55. Kolatkar said this poem first appeared in one of the early numbers of *Quest*, but could not recall the year. Since a complete run of the magazine seems unavailable in any Indian library, one will, for the time being, have to leave it at that. Text from KP. Also written in Marathi; first published in Marathi in *Sabda* (August 1960), as part of a sequence titled 'Kalya kavita' [Black Poems]. Marathi title 'Moolbhoot pinjyaat nar ani nari'; collected in AKK.

In a godforksaken hotel (220)

Written 1954/55. Text from KP. Also written in Marathi; first published in Marathi in *Sabda* (August 1960), as part of a sequence titled 'Kalya kavita' [Black Poems]. Marathi title 'Aadgavchya hotelateel'; collected in AKK. According to Darshan Chhabda, the 'godforsaken hotel' was in Nasik, where she and Kolatkar spent a few days during the early unsettled months of their marriage.

Make Way Poet (221)

Written 1954/55. First published in AAMP, where it says 'Translated by the poet', though no Marathi original exists. The other poems in AAMP which say 'Translated by the poet' and for which there are no Marathi originals are 'Woman', 'Suicide of Rama', 'Teeth' and 'Dreaming of Snakes'. See Appendix II.

The Hag (221)

Written 1959/60. First published in *Dionysus*, vol.1 no. 1 (August 1965). Marathi title 'Therdi'. First published in Marathi in *Aso* (1963); collected in AKK. See Introduction and Appendix II for Kolatkar's comment.

Woman (222)

Written 1960. First published in AAMP. Kolatkar once remarked that this poem ended a period when he had writer's block and was unable to write in either English or Marathi. The period coincided with the time when he was making his meteoric rise in Bombay's advertising world, which he had joined in 1957. See note to 'Make Way Poet'.

Suicide of Rama (223)
Written 1962. First published in AAMP. See note to 'Make Way Poet'.

Irani Restaurant Bombay (224)
Written 1962. First published in AAMP. Marathi title 'Irani'. First published in Marathi in *Aso* (1963); collected in AKK. Kolatkar said that he had combined the interiors of three or four Irani restaurants to create the one described in the poem. For other comments by him, see Introduction and Appendix II.

Visit to a Doctor (225)
Written *c*. 1962. Text from KP.

today i feel i do not belong (226)
Written early 1960s. Text from Design Unit diary/KP. See Introduction.

Teeth (227)
Written *c*. 1963. First published in *Dionysus*, vol.1 no. 1 (August 1965). Three poems in AKK are closely related to 'Teeth': 'Anna', 'Chakki' and 'Chattamatta'. Kolatkar translated the last two as 'Song of the Flour Mill' and 'The Feast'; see 'Poems from the Marathi'. Also see note to 'Make Way Poet' and, for Kolatkar's comment on the poem, Appendix II.

Dreaming of Snakes (228)
Written *c*. 1963. First published in AAMP. See note to 'Make Way Poet'.

my son is dead (229)
Written *c*. 1965. Text from KP. Darshan Chhabda remembers this to be a "found" poem, something that was either told to Kolatkar or something he overheard in a restaurant or in a bar.

My name is Arun Kolatkar (229)
Written *c*. 1967. Text from Design Unit diary/KP. See Introduction.

Directions (230)
Written *c*. 1967. Text from Design Unit diary/KP. See Introduction.

II *Poems in Marathi* (233-74)

FROM *Arun Kolatkarchya Kavita* (1977) (233-59)

One seldom sees a woman (233)
Written *c*. 1960. Marathi title 'Aikti'. First published in Marathi in *Aso* (1963). Text from Design Unit diary/KP.
15 *as an empty frig in a junk shop*: In the Marathi poem, the object in the junk shop is a beat up copper boiler used for heating water. By replacing a 'Maharashtrian' object with a corresponding 'English' one, Kolatkar, in translation theory terms, has 'domesticated' (as opposed to 'foreignised') the translated text. One should add that this is not the only instance of 'domestication' in Kolatkar's translations.

The Fuse (233)
Written *c.* 1960. Marathi title 'Divay'. First published in Marathi in *Aso* (1963).
First published in English in PERI.

Three Cups of Tea (234)
Written 1960. Marathi title 'Main manager ko bola'. First published in Marathi in *Aso* (1963). Text from AAMP and KP. A song version, heavily influenced by blues, is given in Appendix I; also see Appendix II for Kolatkar's comment.
3.2-9 These 8 lines are from a photocopy in KP, where they are typed in the right hand margin, with an arrow to indicate where they are to be inserted. They appear here for the first time.

Song of the Flour Mill (235)
Written mid 1960s. Marathi title 'Chakki'. First published in Marathi in AKK. First published in English in PERI. See note to 'Teeth'.
2.2 *ghatan*: A woman from the Western Ghats.
4.1 *dagdu, thondu or pandu*: Marathi equivalent of Tom, Dick and Harry.

The Turnaround (237)
Written 1967. Marathi title 'Mumbaina bhikes lavla'. First published in Marathi in AKK. Text from KP. See note to 'The Renunciation of the Dog' and Introduction.
7.3 *vishnukranta*: The English word for vishnukranta is speedwheel. A small perennial herb with funnel-shaped bluish flowers, it is distributed throughout India, particularly in open grassy places, and has some medicinal uses.

Biograph (240)
Written 1967. Marathi title 'Charitra'. First published in Marathi in AKK. First published in English in TMIP.

The Wind Song (242)
Written early to mid 1970s. Marathi title 'Kaya danger waren sutlaya'. First published in Marathi in AKK. First published in English in PERI.

Hospital Poems (244)
Written April-June 1965. First published in Marathi in AKK. The 'Hospital Poems', which appear here under a common title, are seven individually titled poems of which Kolatkar translated only the first three and the last. Each poem has an epigraph, which is given in English. Kolatkar was operated for stomach ulcer in March 1965 at Dr Bacha's Nursing Home, Queen's Road, New Marine Lines, Bombay, and the epigraphs, with one exception, are transcribed verbatim from the nurses' private casebook. The epigraphs of the three poems that Kolatkar did not translate are 'Ryles tube removed', 'Passed 4 stools – offensive – unformed – urine scanty', and 'You will have to wear a corset for at least 3 months. – Dr Mehta, FRCS'. The English translation first appeared in the special Kolatkar issue of *Kavi India* (January 1978).
3.5.1 *ramdas*: 17th-century Marathi saint poet.
4.4.1-2 *om mitraya namah / om...*: Traditional salutation to the sun.

Crabs (248)
Written early to mid 1970s. Marathi title 'Khekade'. First published in Marathi in AKK. First published in English in TMIP.

Malkhamb (250)
Written 1975-76. Marathi title 'Malkhamb'. First published in Marathi in AKK. Text from KP. In a note, Kolatkar explains the title: 'It means, literally, "a wrestler's pole". It's a smooth, wooden, vertical pole buried in the ground. A common feature found in all Indian gyms. Used by wrestlers in training and by gymnasts to display their skill.'

Old Newspapers (251)
Written 1975-76. Marathi title 'Raddi'. First published in Marathi in AKK. First published in English in PERI.

Buildings (252)
Written 1975-76. Marathi title 'Buildinga'. First published in Marathi in AKK. Text from KP.

The Blanket (253)
Written 1975-76. Marathi title 'Kambale'. First published in Marathi in AKK. Text from KP.

To a Cloud (254)
Written 1975-76. Marathi title 'Dhag'. First published in Marathi in AKK. First published in English in PERI.

The Feast (256)
Written mid 1960s. Marathi title 'Chattamatta'. First published in Marathi in AKK. Text from KP. See note to 'Teeth'.

Black Handkerchief (257)
Written 1975-76. Marathi title 'Kala roomal'. First published in Marathi in AKK. Text from KP. Though one may not guess this from its instruction manual style, the poem was touched off by Indira Gandhi's emergency (1975-77), when strict censorship laws were in force and Indian writers had to be innovative if they wanted to comment on the state of affairs.

Pictures from a Marathi Alphabet Chart (259)
Written early 1970s. Marathi title 'Takhta'. First published in Marathi in AKK. First published in English in PERI.

FROM *Chirimiri* (2003) (260-74)

In 1974, through his pakhawaj teacher Arjun Shejwal, Kolatkar came in contact with Balwantbua, an eighty-four-year-old bhajan singer and raconteur. They met regularly after that, about once a week, until Balwantbua's death in

1991. On these occasions, Balwantbua would do most of the talking and many of the poems in *Chirimiri* are based on the stories about his extraordinary life that he told Kolatkar. (See 'Crying Mangoes in Colaba' and 'A Highly Prejudiced Account of a Bhajan Session that took place in 1921'.) While he was working on the poems, Kolatkar also began to make notes, in Marathi, of the things that Balwantbua had told him, intending to turn them into poems later. The prose notes eventually became a separate book, *Balwantbua*. It occupied Kolatkar for much of the 1980s, particularly from 1983 to 1985, and those who have read the manuscript (it is unpublished and runs close to 1200 pages) consider it to be his greatest work.

In 1986, when David Davidar of Penguin India, who were to bring out their first titles the following year, approached him for a book, Kolatkar suggested one on his bhajan singer friend and made out a detailed proposal. It consisted of six translated stories from *Balwantbua*, a synopsis, and two notes, 'A bit of background' and 'A bit about the book'. In 'A bit of background' he says how, after their initial few meetings, he 'discovered' that apart from being a great storyteller, Balwantbua was 'a bit of a mime, and something of a stand up comic as well; all of which, put together, made him, in my eyes, nothing less than a whole new art form, all by himself.' What he liked most about Balwantbua, he said, was that 'everything he knew about life had come to him at first hand: from direct observation'. 'He didn't talk about the great events of this century; the two [world] wars, for example, seem to have just passed him by – though horse-drawn trams are remembered fondly and the famous influenza epidemic of 1919... Mostly, he talked about micro-events, or non-events that make up his life – miniature comedies, adventures, misadventures, people he knew, the women in his life – with a sharp eye for the absurdities inherent in situations and the contradictions in human behaviour, looking at the world around him from street level, with his unique sense of humour which equips him with a sort of X-ray vision.' Parts of this almost read like a statement by Kolatkar on his poetic practice, and it is easy to see why in Balwantbua he found a congenial spirit. Penguin were unable to give Kolatkar the sort of advance that would have allowed him to temporarily quit his advertising job and devote himself fulltime to the English *Balwantbua*, and he did not do anything further with the six stories.

Except for 'A Prostitute on a Pilgrimage to Pandharpur Visits the Photographer's Tent during the Annual Ashadhi Fair', Kolatkar did not finalise any of the other translations from *Chirimiri*; see Note on the Text.

The One Who Did Not Go (260)
Written mid 1970s to early 1980s. Marathi title 'Nageli'. First published in Marathi in *Spandan* (1990). Text from KP.

Ambu Invites Vithoba for a Round of Phugadi (261)
Written mid 1970s to early 1980s. Marathi title 'Phugadi'. First published in Marathi in *Spandan* (1990). Text from KP. Ambu, Balwantbua's favourite prostitute, was one of the 107 prostitutes who went with him to the Ashadhi (monsoon) fair held annually in Pandharpur, where there is a famous temple to Vithoba.

377

A Prostitute on a Pilgrimage to Pandharpur Visits the Photographer's Tent during the Annual Ashadi Fair (263)
Written mid 1970s to early 1980s. Marathi title 'Photo'. First published in Marathi in *Spandan* (1990). First published in English in PERI. See note to poem above.

Greetings (264)
Written mid 1970s to early 1980s. Marathi title 'Johar'. Text from KP. 'Johar', or to give its full form, 'Johar mai baap', is how a Mahar traditionally greets a person of a higher caste.

The Left Half (267)
Written mid 1970s to early 1980s. Marathi title 'Vamangi'. First published in Marathi in *Spandan* (1990). Text from KP.

Crying Mangoes in Colaba (267)
Written mid 1970s to early 1980s. Marathi title 'Kolabyachi pheri'. Text from KP.

A Highly Prejudiced Account of a Bhajan Session that took place in 1921 or thereabouts in the Office of Patrick Kelly, the then Police Commissioner of Bombay, at which Govindbua Presented a Marathi Song Written by Dnyaneshwar in the 13th century (269)
Written mid 1970s to early 1980s. Marathi title 'Patrick Kellycha offisat jhaleyla eka prayogik bhajanacha poorvagrahadooshit vrittanta'. Text from KP. In the synopsis he sent David Davidar (see note to *Chirimiri*) Kolatkar says that one of the many things that Balwantbua talks about is 'the bhajan scene in Bombay, as it was in the early decades of this century; about his years of apprenticeship, when he was the sidekick of a major bhajan singer…about a historic bhajan session in the then police commissioner's (Patrick Kelly's) office, which by all accounts was an early attempt at fusion, musically speaking; about how a 13th century Marathi devotional lyric was, specially for the occasion, set to what he describes as a 'band tune', and how it was completely screwed up in the process.'

A Song for Yalloo (271)
Written mid 1970s to early 1980s. Marathi title 'Yalloo'. Text from KP.

Chirimiri (273)
Written mid 1970s to early 1980s. Marathi title 'Chirimiri'. Text from KP. 'Chirimiri' is a small bribe. In the poem, Balwantbua suggests you offer 'chirimiri' to Yama, next time he comes calling.

III *Words for Music* (276-94)

The songs have practically no punctuation, but to indicate a light stop Kolatkar sometimes used additional space, which has been retained in the text. All the songs were written in the late 1960s or early 1970s; see Introduction.

Tape Me Drunk (276)
First published in *Debonair* (March 1977). There is a different version of the song in the Introduction. The *Debonair* version is probably the later of the two.

Third Pasta Lane Breakdown (277)
First published in *Debonair* (March 1977).

Door to Door Blues (278)
First published in *Debonair* (March 1977).

Taxi Song (279)
First published in *Debonair* (March 1977).

Nobody (281)
Text from KP. One of the four songs Kolatkar set to music; see Introduction.
2.3 *shankar*: Name of a colleague in advertising.
2.4 *kooji*: The poet Kersy Katrak's brother.

Hi Constable (282)
Text from KP.

Cold Stone Sober (283)
Text from KP.

A Fraction of a Second Before the Action Starts (284)
Text from KP.

Spinach for Dinner (285)
Text from KP.

Been Working on This Statue (286)
Text from KP.

I Saw a Hair Growing (288)
Text from KP.

What's a Man to Do if a Well Runs Dry (289)
Text from KP.

Molotov Cocktail (290)
Text from KP.

Joe and Bongo Bongo (292)
Text from KP. One of the four songs Kolatkar set to music; see Introduction.

Radio Message from a Quake Hit Town (293)
Text from KP. One of the four songs Kolatkar set to music; see Introduction.
On 31 May 1970 a powerful earthquake was felt across half of Peru, killing

hundreds. It made international headlines and is probably the 'quake' that Kolatkar is referring to in the song.

Poor Man (294)
Text from KP. One of the four songs Kolatkar set to music; see Introduction.

IV *Translations* (297-326)

See note to 'Chaitanya' in *Jejuri* above and Appendix III, 12-14 for Kolatkar's comments on Tukaram; also see Note on the Text.

if death's *(Namdeo)* (297)
Translated late 1960s. Text from KP.

in the beginning *(Namdeo)* (298)
Translated late 1960s. First published in *Vrischik*, vol. 1 no. 11-12 (Sep-Oct 1970).

i eat god *(Janabai)* (299)
Translated late 1960s. First published in *Vrischik*, vol. 1 no. 11-12 (Sep-Oct 1970).

see the void *(Janabai)* (300)
Translated late 1960s. First published in *Vrischik*, vol. 1 no. 11-12 (Sep-Oct 1970).

god my darling *(Janabai)* (301)
Translated late 1960s. Text from KP.

the zoom ant *(Muktabai)* (302)
Translated late 1960s. First published in *Vrischik*, vol. 1 no. 11-12 (Sep-Oct 1970).

wonder of wonders *(Eknath)* (303)
Translated late 1960s. Text from KP.

Who cares for God's man? *(Tukaram)* (304)
Translated 1962. Text from KP. TBAG no.1787.

Lesser *(Tukaram)* (305)
Translated 1962. Text from KP. TBAG no. 993.

I'm tied to this *(Tukaram)* (306)
Translated 1962. Text from KP. TBAG no. 4348.

My body takes on *(Tukaram)* (307)
Translated 1962. Text from KP. TBAG no. 2668.

Don't think I don't *(Tukaram)* (308)
Translated 1962. Text from KP. TBAG no. 567.

What now my son *(Tukaram)* (309)
Translated 1962. Text from KP. TBAG no. 569.

We are the enduring bums *(Tukaram)* (310)
Translated 1962. Text from KP. TBAG no.60.

I followed *(Tukaram)* (311)
Translated 1962. Text from KP. TBAG no. 3855.

Narayan *(Tukaram)* (312)
Translated 1962. Text from KP. TBAG no. 4 (Appendix).

Magnified in every direction *(Tukaram)* (313)
Translated 1962. Text from KP. TBAG no. 3739.

Believe me, saints *(Tukaram)* (314)
Translated 1962. Text from KP. TBAG no. 1334.

There's no percentage *(Tukaram)* (315)
Translated 1962. Text from KP. TBAG no. 1017.

It was a case *(Tukaram)* (316)
Translated 1962. First published in *Poetry India*, vol. 1 no. 1 (Jan-Mar 1966). TBAG no. 1840.

You pawned *(Tukaram)* (317)
Translated 1962. First published in *Poetry India*, vol. 1 no. 1 (Jan-Mar 1966). TBAG no. 4320.

I it was *(Tukaram)* (318)
Translated 1962. First published in *Poetry India*, vol. 1 no. 1 (Jan-Mar 1966). TBAG no. 1337.

Tuka tiptoed *(Tukaram)* (319)
Translated 1962. Text from KP. TBAG no. 505.
3.1 *timeless:* The manuscript has a circle around the word, in pencil. Though marked for revision, no alternative is provided.
3.3 *well-bred:* The word is also written in pencil in the margin, with a question mark against it. No alternative is provided.

Blasted *(Tukaram)* (320)
Translated 1962. Text from KP. TBAG no. 4306.
4.4: *Pandurang*: Or Vitthal, Vithal, or Vithoba, a form of Krishna or Vishnu, worshipped at Pandharpur.

Tuka is stark raving mad *(Tukaram)* (321)
Translated 1962. First published in *Poetry India*, vol. 1 no. 1 (Jan-Mar 1966).
TBAG no. 2869.

I've had my days *(Tukaram)* (322)
Translated 1962. First published in *Poetry India*, vol. 1 no. 1 (Jan-Mar 1966).
TBAG no. 4024.

Lacking the guile *(Tukaram)* (323)
Translated 1962. First published in *Poetry India*, vol. 1 no. 1 (Jan-Mar 1966).
TBAG no. 272.

Without seeing a thing *(Tukaram)* (324)
Translated 1962. First published in *Poetry India*, vol. 1 no. 1 (Jan-Mar 1966).
TBAG no.249.
2.3-4: The manuscript has a curly bracket against these lines, followed by a
question mark that is crossed out.

What will I eat now *(Tukaram)* (325)
Translated 1962. First published in *Poetry India*, vol. 1 no. 1 (Jan-Mar 1966).
TBAG no. 388.

Harvest done *(Tukaram)* (326)
Translated 1962. First published in *Poetry India*, vol. 1 no. 1 (Jan-Mar 1966).
TBAG no. 200.
4.1: In both printed text and manuscript, the line is given as 'We are all about'.
The decision to amend it is the editor's. The manuscript has a curly bracket
against this line and the one following it, 4.2, marking them out for revision,
which was never made.

V *The Boatride* (329-35)

Written 1963. First published in *damn you*, no. 6 (1968).
6.21-22: *Goa*, which had been a Portuguese colony since the early 16th cen-
tury, was liberated in December 1961.

APPENDICES

I *Poems* (338-343)

an alfabet for darshan (338)
Written 1960/1. Text from photocopy made available by Darshan Chhabda.
Kolatkar originally wrote the poem on 26 sheets of paper and mailed it in 26
envelopes to Darshan who, at the time, was visiting her family in Ahmedabad.
The envelopes and their contents are now lost, but Kolatkar subsequently
wrote out the poem in a copybook. He forgot to include the letter W when
he did so, which is why the poem, as it appears here, has only 25 'alfabets'.

5.3 *ellis bridge*: One of the bridges over the Sabarmati in Ahmedabad.

5.7 *eddy duchin*: The Eddy Duchin Story (1956), a biopic, starring Tyrone Power and Kim Novak, based on the life of the 1930s-40s pianist and band-leader Eddy Duchin.

7.3 *glendora*: A popular song written by Ray Stanley and recorded in 1956. Glendora, who 'works in the window of a big department stor-a!' is a manne-quin. The song's refrain is 'O' Glendora...I wanna see more of you!'

11.3 *kotex*: Well-known brand of feminine hygiene products.

11.5 *kauphy*: Tamil word for 'coffee'. Kolatkar and Darshan spent the early years of their marriage in Chennai.

12.5 *lumumba*: Patrice Lumumba (1925-61), African nationalist leader and the first prime minister of the Republic of Congo (the former Belgian Congo, later Republic of Zaïre and now the Democratic Republic of Congo). His assassin-ation led to protests throughout the world.

14.3 *nahi tar kai*: Marathi phrase which means 'Isn't it so?'

16.5 *pearl chowdhry*: Pearl Padamsee (1931-2000), Bombay theatre director and film actress.

19.1 *s.r. bhat*: English lecturer in the Ahmedabad college where Darshan had been a student; the girls had a crush on him.

Three Cups of Tea: Song version (342)
Written late 1960s/early 1970s. Text from KP. See note to 'Three Cups of Tea'.

awards have many uses (343)
Written 1999. Text from KP. Kolatkar was given the Bank of India award for literature in 1999; among the other awardees that year were Akbar Padamsee (*b.* 1928) for painting and Sham Lal (1912-2007) for journalism. The mock speech was of course never delivered.

II *From an Undated Sheet* (344)

The comments are from a single typewritten sheet in KP, probably dating from the late 1960s.

III *Making love to a poem* (345-53)

The jottings, with occasionally a passage copied from a book or journal, are made on small unnumbered sheets, of which Kolatkar always kept a stock handy. They don't have any dates but seem to be from the 1980s. Most of them are typed, though some are in holograph. While transcribing them, I have retained the repetitions as well as the line breaks and the extra spaces he sometimes introduced between words or phrases. With some exceptions, only the jottings that have to do with translation or bilingualism are included.

12.7 *Salo Malo:* a fictional character in Prabhat Film Company's 1936 classic *Sant Tukaram*. He tried to pass off Tukaram's poems as his own.

Milton Keynes UK
Ingram Content Group UK Ltd.
UKHW041042190924
448527UK00001B/20

9 781852 248536